PAGAN AND CHRISTIAN
IN AN AGE OF ANXIETY

E. R. DODDS received his education at Campbell College, Belfast, and University College, Oxford. He was lecturer in Classics at University College, Reading, from 1919 to 1924; Professor of Greek at the University of Birmingham 1924 to 1936; and since 1936 has been Regius Professor of Greek, now emeritus, at the University of Oxford.

PAGAN AND CHRISTIAN IN AN AGE OF ANXIETY

SOME ASPECTS OF RELIGIOUS EXPERIENCE
FROM MARCUS AURELIUS TO
CONSTANTINE

BY

E. R. DODDS

The Norton Library
W · W · NORTON & COMPANY · INC ·
NEW YORK

DIS MANIBUS
ARTHUR DARBY NOCK

Books That Live
The Norton imprint on a book means that in the publisher's
estimation it is a book not for a single season but for the years.
W. W. Norton & Company, Inc.

ISBN   0   393   00545   3

PRINTED IN THE UNITED STATES OF AMERICA

6 7 8 9 0

CONTENTS

PREFACE

THIS little book is based on a course of four lectures which I had the honour of delivering in May 1963 in the Queen's University, Belfast, on the invitation of the Wiles Foundation. The lectures are printed substantially as they were spoken, save for a few additions and corrections. They were addressed to a general audience, and I hope that in their printed form they will be of interest to the general reader who has no specialised knowledge of ancient thought or of Christian theology. I have, however, supplemented them with footnotes which specify the evidence on which my statements are based, and develop some additional arguments and speculations.

My thanks are due in the first place to the Wiles Foundation and to all those who took personal trouble to make my visit to Belfast an agreeable experience: in particular to Dr Michael Grant, Vice-Chancellor of the Queen's University, and to Mrs Grant; to Mrs Austen Boyd; and to Professor Michael Roberts. I am most grateful also to those scholars who attended my lectures as guests of the Foundation and discussed them with me at the colloquia which followed, namely A. H. Armstrong, H. Butterfield, Henry Chadwick, R. Duncan-Jones, Pierre Hadot, A. H. M. Jones, A. D. Momigliano, H. W. Parke, Audrey Rich, S. Weinstock and G. Zuntz. Here and there in this book they will, I hope, recognise echoes of their individual contributions. But the main value of these colloquia lay in the informal interchange of ideas between representatives of several disciplines which even today are still too often pursued in timid isolation.

In preparing my manuscript for publication I have received generous help from two friends who are experts in fields of which my own knowledge is very incomplete: Henry Chadwick in patristics and George Devereux in psychology. They have saved me from a number of errors; for those which remain my native obstinacy is alone responsible.

E. R. D.

Oxford
October 1963

Since the above was written a version of these lectures has been delivered as the Eitrem Lectures for 1964 in the University of Oslo. I must take this opportunity to thank Professor Leiv Amundsen, Professor Eiliv Skard, Dr Egil Wyller and others for generous hospitality and helpful criticism.

E. R. D.

September 1964

KEY TO REFERENCES

Titles of works frequently cited in the notes are given in abridged form. Full details are listed below.

Cohn, *Pursuit of the Millennium*: N. Cohn, *The Pursuit of the Millennium*, 1957.

Daniélou, *Origen*: J. Daniélou, *Origen*, Eng. trans., 1955.

Dodds, *Greeks*: E. R. Dodds, *The Greeks and the Irrational*, 1951.

Festugière, *Personal Religion*: A.-J. Festugière, *Personal Religion among the Greeks* (Sather Classical Lectures, 1954).

Festugière, *Révélation*: A.-J. Festugière, *La Révélation d'Hermès Trismégiste*, 1944-54.

Grant, *Gnosticism*: R. M. Grant, *Gnosticism and Early Christianity*, 1959.

Harnack, *Mission*: A. Harnack, *Mission and Expansion of Christianity*, Eng. trans., 1908.

Jonas, *Gnosis*: H. Jonas, *Gnosis und spätantiker Geist*, 1934.

Kirk, *Vision*: K. E. Kirk, *The Vision of God*, 1931.

Labriolle, *Crise*: P. de Labriolle, *La Crise Montaniste*, 1913.

Labriolle, *Réaction*: P. de Labriolle, *La Réaction païenne*, 1934.

Les Sources de Plotin: Entretiens Hardt, V, 1960.

Miura-Stange, *Celsus u. Origenes*: A. Miura-Stange, *Celsus und Origenes, das Gemeinsame ihrer Weltanschauung*, 1926.

Momigliano, *Conflict*: A. Momigliano (ed.), *The Conflict between Paganism and Christianity in the Fourth Century*, 1963.

Nilsson, *Gesch.*: M. P. Nilsson, *Geschichte der griechischen Religion*, 1941-50.

Nock, *Conversion*: A. D. Nock, *Conversion*, 1933.

Reitzenstein, *Hell. Wund.*: R. Reitzenstein, *Hellenistische Wundererzählungen*, 1906.

Stace, *Mysticism and Philosophy*: W. T. Stace, *Mysticism and Philosophy*, 1960.

Key to References

Völker, *Quellen*: W. Völker, *Quellen zur Geschichte der Christlichen Gnosis*, 1932.

Walzer, *Galen*: R. Walzer, *Galen on Jews and Christians*, 1949.

Zaehner, *Mysticism*: R. C. Zaehner, *Mysticism Sacred and Profane*, paperback edn., 1961.

References to Plotinus

In references of the form 1, ii, 3.45, the last figure refers to the lines of Henry and Schwyzer's edition, except in the case of *Ennead* VI where the lineation is Bréhier's, the Henry–Schwyzer edition not being yet available.

I have it in me so much nearer home
To scare myself with my own desert places.

ROBERT FROST

CHAPTER I

MAN AND THE MATERIAL WORLD

The meaningless absurdity of life is the only incontestable knowledge accessible to man. TOLSTOI

THE Wiles Trust, to which this book owes its origin, was established 'to promote the study of the history of civilisation and to encourage the extension of historical thinking into the realm of general ideas'. In what way the present volume of lectures can hope to serve that aim I can perhaps best indicate by quoting two remarks made by eminent ancient historians. In the last chapter of his *Social and Economic History of the Roman Empire*, after examining and criticising the numerous theories, political, economic and biological, by which men have sought to explain the decline of the Empire, Rostovtzeff finally turned to psychological explanation. He expressed the view that a change in people's outlook on the world 'was one of the most potent factors'; and he added that further investigation of this change is 'one of the most urgent tasks in the field of ancient history'. My second quotation is from the closing chapter of Professor Nilsson's *Geschichte der griechischen Religion*. He writes: 'The study of the syncretism of late antiquity which has been actively pursued in recent de-

cades has concerned itself mainly with beliefs and doctrines, while the spiritual soil from which these growths
arose and drew their nourishment has been touched on
only in passing and in general terms; yet that is the heart
of the matter, its weightiest element.' And he goes on to
point out that for a study of the religious experience of
late antiquity 'in William James's sense' there is abundant
material available.[1]

I hope that these two quotations sufficiently suggest
what I am attempting to do in these lectures. Fully to
explain the change of mental outlook and its relationship
to the material decline would be a task far beyond my
competence; but within the particular field to which
Nilsson points I shall try to contribute something towards a better understanding of what was happening, and
even—in certain cases—of why it happened. These are
lectures on religious experience in the Jamesian sense.[2] If
I touch on the development of pagan philosophical theory
or of Christian religious dogma, I shall do so only to provide a background for the personal experience of individuals. With the external forms of worship I shall not deal
at all. I shall not, for example, discuss the so-called
'mystery-religions' and their supposed influence on Christian ritual, since with rare exceptions they provide nothing germane to my present purpose: apart from the
controversial statements of Christian Fathers, the evidence

---

[1] M. Rostovtzeff, *Social and Economic History of the Roman Empire* (1926),
p. 486; Nilsson, *Gesch.* II, p. 682.

[2] James defined religion, for his purposes, as 'the feelings, acts and experiences of individual men in their solitude, so far as they apprehend themselves
to stand in relation to whatever they may consider the divine'. *The Varieties of
Religious Experience* (1902), Lecture ii, p. 50 (Fontana Library edition).

for them is chiefly inscriptional, and inscriptions seldom tell us much about the underlying personal experience. The most striking exception is the famous account of Isiac initiation in the last book of Apuleius' *Metamorphoses*; and that has been so thoroughly discussed by Nock, Festugière[1] and others that I have nothing to add.

Even with these limitations the subject proposed by Rostovtzeff and Nilsson is still far too wide. A story which begins with Philo and St Paul and ends with Augustine and Boethius is much too long to be told in four lectures, even if I were competent to tell the whole of it. I have therefore judged it best to concentrate my attention on the crucial period between the accession of Marcus Aurelius and the conversion of Constantine, the period when the material decline was steepest and the ferment of new religious feelings most intense. In calling it 'an Age of Anxiety' I have in mind both its material and its moral insecurity; the phrase was coined by my friend W. H. Auden, who applied it to our own time, I suppose with a similar dual reference. The practice of chopping history into convenient lengths and calling them 'periods' or 'ages' has of course its drawbacks. Strictly speaking, there are no periods in history, only in historians; actual history is a smoothly flowing continuum, a day following a day. And even when hindsight enables us to cut it through at a critical point, there is always a time-lag and an overlap. When Marcus Aurelius came to the throne no bell rang to warn the world that the *pax Romana* was about to end and be succeeded by an age of barbarian invasions, bloody civil wars, recurrent epidemics, galloping

[1] Nock, *Conversion*, ch. ix; Festugière, *Personal Religion*, ch. v.

3

inflation and extreme personal insecurity. For a long time the majority of individuals must have continued to think and feel as they had always thought and felt; the adjustment to the new situation could only be gradual. More surprisingly, a time-lag of the opposite kind also occurs: moral and intellectual insecurity can anticipate its material counterpart. C. G. Jung remarks somewhere that 'long before 1933 there was already a faint smell of burning in the air'.[1] In the same way we can recognise a foretaste of things to come in the last chapter of the treatise *On the Sublime*, in certain passages of Epictetus and Plutarch, and most clearly of all in Gnosticism, of which the best-known representatives—Saturninus, Basileides, Valentinus and (if we count him a Gnostic) Marcion—constructed their systems in the prosperous years of the Antonine peace.[2] For these reasons I shall treat my chronological limits with some elasticity where the evidence demands it.

One other confession and I shall have done with these

[1] C. G. Jung, *Essays on Contemporary Events* (Eng. trans. 1947), p. 51. Cf. *ibid.*, p. 69: 'Long before the Hitler era, in fact before the first World War, there were already symptoms of the mental change which was taking place in Europe. The mediaeval picture of the world was breaking up and the metaphysical authority which was set above this world was fast disappearing.'

[2] [Longinus], *De sublim.*, 44.6 ff., the world enslaved to passion; Epict., 3. 13.9 ff., the external security of the *pax Romana* contrasted with the essential insecurity of the human condition; Plut. *De superstit.*, 7, 168 CD, on the new sense of sin (cf. my paper in *Greece and Rome*, 1933, pp. 101 ff.), and the radical dualism of *Is. et Os.*, 45–6, 369 B ff. On the chronological difficulty of the view that Gnosticism was simply a reaction to material hardship see Jonas, *Gnosis*, I, pp. 64 f. In the same way Erich Fromm's speculations in *The Dogma of Christ*, 1930 (Eng. trans., 1963), founder on the rock of chronology; he makes third-century social conditions responsible for shifts of dogma which had in fact set in much earlier.

preliminaries. The historian's interpretation of this period is inevitably coloured in some degree by his own religious beliefs. It is therefore right that I should declare my interest, so that readers may make the appropriate allowances. It is in fact a kind of disinterest. As an agnostic I cannot share the standpoint of those who see the triumph of Christianity as the divine event to which the whole creation moved. But equally I cannot see it as the blotting out of the sunshine of Hellenism by what Proclus called 'the barbarian theosophy'.[1] If there is more about pagans in these lectures than about Christians, it is not because I like them better; it is merely because I know them better. I stand outside this particular battle, though not above it: I am interested less in the issues which separated the combatants than in the attitudes and experiences which bound them together.

In this first chapter I shall discuss general attitudes to the world and the human condition; in the second and third, some specific types of experience. Joseph Bidez described our period as one in which 'Men were ceasing to observe the external world and to try to understand it, utilize it or improve it. They were driven in upon themselves. . . . The idea of the beauty of the heavens and of the world went out of fashion and was replaced by that of the Infinite.'[2] How did this change come about? Was Freud right in connecting it with 'the low estimation put upon earthly life by Christian doctrine'?[3]

Let us start by reminding ourselves of the physical pic-

[1] Proclus, *In Remp.*, II, 255.21 Kroll.
[2] Joseph Bidez, *C.A.H.*, XII, p. 629.
[3] Sigmund Freud, *Civilization and its Discontents* (Eng. trans., 1930), p. 45.

ture of the cosmos which later antiquity inherited from Aristotle and the Hellenistic astronomers.[1] The earth was a globe suspended in space at the centre of a system of concentric moving spheres. First came the envelope of thick and murky terrestrial atmosphere which reached as far as the moon; beyond the moon were the successive spheres of the sun and the five planets; beyond these again the eighth sphere, composed of fiery ether, purest of material elements, which in its daily revolution about the earth carried round with it the fixed stars. The whole vast structure was seen as the expression of a divine order; as such, it was felt to be beautiful and worshipful; and because it was self-moving it was thought to be alive or informed by a living spirit. So much was common ground to all the philosophical schools save the Epicureans, and for most men educated in the Greek tradition it remained common ground throughout our period and beyond it. But while the parts of this cosmos were believed to be linked together by *sympatheia*, an unconscious community of life, the status and value of the parts was by no means uniform. Across the cosmic map Aristotle, following hints in Plato, had drawn a line which came to be generally accepted: above the line, beyond the moon, lay the unvarying heavens where the stars moved, 'rank on rank, The army of unalterable law'; below it lay the sublunar world, the domain of chance, mutability and death. And in this glittering house of many mansions the earth appeared as the meanest mansion of all: it was held to be

[1] On the general religious influence of this world-picture see Nilsson, 'The New Conception of the Universe in Late Greek Paganism', *Eranos*, 44 (1946), pp. 20 ff.

compact of the mere dregs and sediment of the universe, the cold, heavy, impure stuff whose weight had caused it to sink to the centre.

As time went on, this traditional antithesis between the celestial world and the terrestrial was more and more heavily emphasised,[1] and it was increasingly used to point a moral. In the recurrent *topos* of the flight of the soul through the universe—imagined as taking place in a dream, or after death, or sometimes just in waking contemplation—we can trace a growing contempt for all that may be done and suffered beneath the moon. That the earth is physically tiny in comparison with the vastness of space had been noted by the astronomers: it was no more than a pinpoint, a στιγμή or *punctum*, on the cosmic map.[2] And the moralists early used this observation as the text for a sermon on the vanity of human wishes: it appears in Cicero, in Seneca, in Celsus, in pseudo-Aristotle *De mundo*, and in Lucian's parody of a celestial voyage, the *Icaromenippus*.[3] That is perhaps no more than literary fashion; all these authors may be copying from a Greek model which is now lost. But the writer who

[1] Logically, Christianity, holding as it did that heaven and earth were alike the creation of God and alike perishable, might have been expected to deny the antithesis or at least attenuate it. But it seems that only John Philoponus in the sixth century attempted this, and his attempt made no impression: the old equation, 'celestial' = 'divine', was too firmly established in the human imagination. See S. Sambursky, *The Physical World of Late Antiquity* (1962), ch. vi.

[2] Geminus (c. 70 B.C.), 16.29, p. 176.7 ff. Manit.; Cleomedes, 1.11.56, p. 102.21 ff. Ziegler. Cf. Festugière, *Révélation*, II, pp. 449 ff.

[3] Cic., *Somn. Scip.*, 3.16; Sen., *N.Q.* i, *praef.* 8; Celsus *apud* Orig. *c. Cels.*, 4.85; [Ar.], *De mundo*, 1, 391 a 18 ff.; Lucian, *Icar.*, 18, where the richest landowners are seen as farming 'a single Epicurean atom'. Most of these passages are quoted in full by Festugière, *loc. cit.* Cf. also Plotinus, III, ii, 8.6, with Theiler's note. For celestial voyages in general see most recently J. D. P. Bolton, *Aristeas of Proconnesus* (1962), ch. vii.

really makes the thought his own, detaching it from the artificial context of the celestial voyage and using it in many variations with a quite new intensity, is Marcus Aurelius. As the earth is a pinpoint in infinite space, so the life of man is a pinpoint in infinite time, a knife-edge between two eternities—στιγμὴ τοῦ αἰῶνος.[1] His activities are 'smoke and nothingness'; his prizes are 'a bird flying past, vanished before we can grasp it'. The clash of armies is 'the quarrel of puppies over a bone'; the pomp of Marcus's own Sarmatian triumph is the self-satisfaction of a spider which has caught a fly.[2] For Marcus this is not empty rhetoric: it is a view of the human condition, and it is meant in deadly earnest.

Associated with it in Marcus is the feeling that man's activity is not only unimportant, it is also in some sense not quite real. This feeling was expressed in another ancient *topos*—the comparison, staled for us by much repetition, of the world to a stage and men to actors or marionettes. It has a long history, starting from two passages in Plato's *Laws*, where we are told that 'men and women are puppets chiefly, having in them only a small portion of reality'; whether God designed them as playthings only, or for some more serious purpose, remains in

---

[1] M. Ant., 6.36. Cf. 4.3.3 τὸ χάος τοῦ ἐφ' ἑκάτερα ἀπείρου αἰῶνος: 9.32; 10.17; 12.32. The transference of the idea from space to time is again not new (cf. Sen., *Epist.* 49.3; Plut. [?] *De educ.*, 17, 13 A, and *Cons. ad Apoll.*, 17, 111 C). But it is expressed by Marcus with a new vehemence of conviction; and the personal character of his notebooks makes them better evidence for 'the feelings of an individual man in his solitude' than the letters of Seneca, the essays of Plutarch or the sermons of Epictetus, all of which were designed for a public audience.

[2] M. Ant., 10.31; 6.15; 5.33; 10.10, a sardonic allusion to the triumph celebrated in A.D. 176.

doubt.[1] After Plato the image was exploited by the early Cynics and Sceptics: for Bion of Borysthenes, Chance (τύχη) is the authoress of the drama; for Anaxarchus and Monimus what we call reality is a stage set, and our experience of it is no more than a dream or a delusion.[2] The Stoics, from Chrysippus onwards, use the comparison more conventionally, to point the banal moral that it takes all sorts to make a world, or to emphasise, as Seneca and Epictetus do, that one should make the best even of a very minor part.[3] It is only in Marcus Aurelius that the suggestion of unreality reappears, for example where he jots down a series of images for human life, beginning with 'stage plays and the vain pomp of processions' and ending with 'puppets jerking on a string'; in between come sham fights, the throwing of bones to puppies or crumbs to fish, the futile industry of ants and the futile scurrying of panic-stricken mice. Elsewhere he speaks of the whole of our perceptual life as 'a dream and a delirium'.[4] Much the same feeling underlies the long and

[1] Plato, *Laws*, 804 B, 644 D-E. Cf. Dodds, *Greeks*, pp. 214 f., 229; and H. D. Rankin in *Eranos*, 60 (1962), pp. 127-31.

[2] Teles, p. 5.1 Hense; Sext. Emp., *Adv. math.*, 7.88.

[3] Chrysippus, *SVF* II, 1181; Sen., *Epist.* 77.20; Epict., 1.29.39-43; 4.1. 165; 4.7.13. And so also Clement of Alexandria, *Strom.*, 7.11.65. On the various applications of the comparison see R. Helm, *Lucian und Menipp* (1906), pp. 45 ff.

[4] M. Ant., 7.3; 2.17.1, τὰ δὲ τῆς ψυχῆς ὄνειρος καὶ τῦφος, where ψυχή must be understood as excluding νοῦς (cf. the threefold division of the personality at 12.3). For worldly existence as dreaming see also 6.31. The comparison of human life to a dream was familiar from classical Greek poetry (Pindar, *Pyth.*, 8.95 ff., Aesch., *P.V.*, 547 ff., Aristoph., *Birds*, 687), but in our period it is reiterated by philosophers with a new earnestness, partly on the basis of Plato, *Rep.*, 476 C. It appears in Marcus' contemporaries, Albinus (*Epitome*, 14.3) and Maximus of Tyre (10.6), but is most fully developed by Plotinus, III, vi, 6.65 ff., and Porphyry, *De abst.*, 1.27 f.: to them the thought has become more than a metaphor. Further examples are quoted by

9

splendid passage where Plotinus in his last years, drawing both on Plato and on the Stoics, interprets the grandeurs and miseries of human life in terms of a stage performance. For him, as for the aged Plato, man's earnest is God's play, performed in the world-theatre by 'fair and lovely living puppets'—puppets who mistake themselves for men and suffer accordingly, though in truth they are but external shadows of the inner man, the only truly existent, truly substantial person.[1] This is linked with Plotinus' general doctrine that action is everywhere 'a shadow of contemplation and an inferior substitute for it.'[2] When cities are sacked, their men massacred, their women raped, it is but a transitory moment in the endless drama: other and better cities will arise one day, and the children conceived in crime may prove better men than their fathers.[3] That seems to be his final word on the tragic history of his time.

From Plotinus this attitude of contemptuous resignation was transmitted to the later Neoplatonic school, Christian as well as pagan. To Gregory of Nyssa, for

Merkelbach, *Roman und Mysterium* (1962), p. 315, n. 2. Especially striking is the intensification of the comparison in the recently published *Evangelium Veritatis*, a Valentinian document, where worldly life is elaborately likened not to a dream but to a nightmare (p. 28.26–30.14 Malinine–Puech–Quispel).

[1] Plot., III, ii, 15. The theme is further elaborated in chs. 16–18 with reference to the problem of free will (the puppet theory must not be used to evade responsibility). It is significant, as Professor Armstrong points out to me, that in Plotinus only the 'outer man' is a puppet, whereas in the *Laws* the most serious human activities are treated as a kind of play (803 C: cf. *Epin.*, 980 A). On the status of the Plotinian 'inner man' see below, ch. III, pp. 83f.

[2] Plot., III, viii, 4.

[3] Plot., III, ii, 18.15 ff. In A.D. 269, about the time when Plotinus wrote these words, Byzantium was looted by its own garrison; a few years earlier Autun had been sacked by a mob of soldiers and peasants. Cf. also I, iv, 7.18 ff., the eloquent passage from which Augustine quoted at the siege of Hippo (Possidius, *Vit. Aug.* 28).

example, human affairs are but the play of children building sand castles which are promptly washed away; as
Father Daniélou says, his entire work is penetrated by a
deep feeling of the unreality of the sensible world, which
he calls γοητεία, a magical illusion, echoing a phrase of
Porphyry.[1] And Augustine in turn declares that 'this life
is nothing but the comedy of the human race'.[2] From
him and from Boethius the image passed into the reper-
tory of later moralists and poets, where its long career has
been studied by Ernst Curtius.[3] But even in antiquity it
would be a mistake to assume that such an attitude was
confined to philosophers and divines. Stripped of all
metaphysical overtones, it is movingly expressed in a
well-known epigram by the pagan poet Palladas:

σκηνὴ πᾶς ὁ βίος καὶ παίγνιον· ἢ μάθε παίζειν
τὴν σπουδὴν μεταθείς, ἢ φέρε τὰς ὀδύνας.[4]

The world's a stage and life's a toy:
Dress up and play your part;
Put every serious thought away—
Or risk a broken heart.

Palladas lived in the fourth century; but already in the third
there must have been many who shared his feeling. Con-

---

[1] Greg. Nyss., *P.G.*, 44, 628 C, 428 C. Cf. Plot., IV, iii, 17.27, πεδηθεῖσαι
γοητείας δεσμοῖς; Porph., *De abst.*, 1.28, τὸ γοήτευμα τῆς ἐνταῦθ᾽ ἡμῶν
διατριβῆς; and J. Daniélou, *Platonisme et théologie mystique* (1944), p. 182.
[2] Augustine, *Enarr. ad Ps.*, 127. Porphyry calls it a tragi-comedy, *Ad
Marc.*, 2.
[3] E. R. Curtius, *European Literature and the Latin Middle Ages* (Eng. trans.,
1953), pp. 138–44.
[4] *Anth. Pal.*, 10.72.

sider the words of Cyprian, who was Plotinus' contemporary.[1] 'The world today,' he says, 'speaks for itself: by the evidence of its decay it announces its dissolution. The farmers are vanishing from the countryside, commerce from the sea, soldiers from the camps; all honesty in business, all justice in the courts, all solidarity in friendship, all skill in the arts, all standards in morals—all are disappearing.' We must allow for some rhetorical exaggeration here; but I think historians will agree that Cyprian's description is on the whole a true one. To identify oneself with such a world, to take it seriously as a place to live and labour in, must have demanded more courage than the average man possessed: better treat it as an illusion or a bad joke, and avoid heartbreak.

Marcus Aurelius, Plotinus and Palladas were men brought up in the Greek tradition, who thought and felt within the limits set by that tradition. They could recognise with Plato that this sublunar world 'is of necessity haunted by evil',[2] and could feel that man's activity in it is something of a secondary order, less than serious, less

---

[1] Cyprian, *Ad Demetrianum*, 3 (*CSEL*, III, i, 352). Cf. Arnobius' horrifying description of the human condition (*Adv. nat.*, 2.45–6), and the gloomy predictions of Origen, *Comm. in Matt.*, series 36: 'This vast and wonderful creation of the world . . . must of necessity before it decays grow feeble. Hence the earth will more often be shaken by earthquakes, and the atmosphere will become pestilential, generating a contagious malignity.' He goes on to predict food shortages leading to predatory raids and class warfare; at the same time he expects 'a deficiency of right-minded men'. It seems likely that he is prophesying to some extent *post eventum*. For many Christian minds such pessimism was encouraged by, and found its deepest expression in, the conviction that the entire world was scheduled for early destruction. We may compare, *mutatis mutandis*, the way in which today an unconscious 'death-wish' finds satisfaction in picturing the destruction to be wrought by a future atomic war.

[2] Plato, *Theaet.*, 176 A.

than fully real—in fact 'absurd' in the sense which Camus gave to that term. But no Stoic or Aristotelian, and no orthodox Platonist, could condemn the cosmos as a whole. Where we meet such condemnation we must suspect that it derives ultimately from a source farther east, a dualism more radical than Plato's. The visible cosmos *as a whole* could only be called evil in contrast with some invisible Good Place or Good Person outside and beyond the cosmos: radical dualism implies transcendence.[1] Stoicism recognised no such place or person: it was a one-storey system. Platonism of course did; but for orthodox Platonism the relation of the visible cosmos to the world of Forms was one of dependence, not of opposition: it was in the words of the *Timaeus* 'an image of the intelligible, a perceptible god, supreme in greatness and excellence, in beauty and perfection, single in its kind and one'.[2] Where we find the visible cosmos set in opposition to God, the opposing principle may be described in any or all of three ways: (1) as Matter or 'Darkness', conceived as a substance not created by God and resistant to his will; (2) as Fate, whose agents are the planetary demons, the Keepers of the Seven Gates which cut off the world from God; or finally (3) as a personal evil principle, the lord of this world and in some versions its creator. All these notions are found in various combinations in Christian Gnosticism; some of them were held by orthodox Christians; but they had also a wide currency among pagans. And all of them are attested well before our period, so

[1] Cf. S. Pétrement, *Le Dualisme dans l'histoire de la philosophie et des religions* (1946), p. 105.
[2] Plato, *Tim.*, 92 C.

that they cannot be dismissed as mere by-products of the Age of Anxiety.

The conception of Matter as an independent principle and the source of evil has both Greek and oriental roots. The doxographers attribute it to Pythagoras,[1] and authority could be found for it in certain passages of Plato;[2] its strongest champion was the Neopythagorean Numenius.[3] On the other hand the early Gnostic Basileides presents it as the wisdom of the barbarians, i.e. the Persians.[4] Unlike the other two views, it did not involve a total devaluation of the cosmos, which contains at least some portion, however exiguous, of Form as well as Matter, of light as well as darkness. But its irreducible dualism ran counter to the main Greek tradition: Plotinus could accept the equation of Matter with evil only by reducing both to the status of marginal products, the limiting point of the outgoing from the Absolute.

The remaining conceptions are apparently oriental in origin. The Keepers of the Gates would seem to derive ultimately from the Babylonian cult of planetary gods, although at some point in their long history they have suffered a transformation from the status of high gods to that of maleficent demons.[5] From the first century on-

[1] H. Diels, *Dox. gr.*, p. 302.

[2] Whether the identification of Matter as the cause of evil is in fact Platonic is a question still actively debated: for a summary of opposing views see F. P. Hager, 'Die Materie und das Böse im antiken Platonismus', *Mus. Helv.*, 19 (1962), pp. 73 ff.

[3] Numenius T.30 Leemans = Chalcidius *In Tim.*, 295–9. It has been conjectured that the Mandaean demon Ur, the Power of Darkness who swallows souls, is simply the Greek ὕλη (F. C. Burkitt, *Church and Gnosis*, 1932, p. 116).

[4] Basileides, fr. 1 (Völker, *Quellen*, p. 38) = Hegemonius, *Acta Archelai*, 67.4–12, p. 96.10 ff. Beeson.

[5] According to W. Bousset, *Hauptprobleme der Gnosis* (1907), p. 55, this 'down-

wards the mass of men—Jew or Christian, Gnostic or pagan—admit their maleficent power. They are the *archontes* of the Gnostics, the *cosmocratores* of the Epistle to the Ephesians, the Seven Governors of the Hermetist, 'whose government is called Destiny'; that they were feared by Christians as well as pagans is attested by Origen and by Augustine.[1] Even in our period, however, the best minds denied the tyranny. Plotinus wrote an essay to show that while in virtue of the universal *sympatheia* the stars may *indicate* the future, they cannot *determine* it —and when shortly afterwards he died of an unpleasant disease, the astrologers saw in it the vengeance of the offended star-demons. Similarly Origen denied the causative power of the stars while admitting that they could function as signs (did not God say, 'Let there be lights in the firmament of the heaven . . . and let them be for signs'?). It was left for Augustine, arguing from the case of twins, to deny the truth of astrology altogether.[2]

grading' (or rather, moral transvaluation) was a consequence of the Persian conquest of Babylon in the sixth century B.C. But see the doubts of H. Jonas, *Gnosis*, I, pp. 28 ff.; S. Pétrement, *Le Dualisme chez Platon, les Gnostiques et les Manichéens* (1947), pp. 153 f.; Nilsson, *Gesch.*, II, p. 573. The devaluation of the planetary gods looks more like a consequence of the general devaluation of the cosmos; it is the latter that has to be accounted for. The Manichaeans represented the transformation in mythical form: the five 'luminous gods', sons of the Primordial Man, lost their intelligence when their substance was devoured by the powers of darkness, and became 'like a man bitten by a mad dog or a snake' (A. Adam, *Texte zum Manichäismus*, (1954), p. 17).

[1] Ephes. vi. 12; *Corp. Herm.*, i, 9 (cf. xvi, 16); Origen *apud* Eus., *Praep., Ev.*, 6.11.1; Augustine, *Civ. Dei*, 5.1. See also the many passages collected by Mayor in his note on Juvenal 14.248.

[2] Plot., II, iii; Firmicus Maternus, 1.7.18; Origen *apud* Eus., *Praep.Ev.*, 6. 11.1; Augustine, *Civ. Dei*, Book 5, and *De Gen. ad litt.*, 2.17. Origen and Plotinus appear to draw on a common pagan source: see R. Cadiou, *La Jeunesse d' Origène* (1935) pp. 206–12. The argument from twins is traditional (Cic., *Div.*, 2.90; Origen, *Philocalia*, 23.18), but it was Augustine who developed it most fully and effectively.

In the third view, which saw the sensible world as the domain or even the product of an evil personal power, Plutarch recognised, no doubt rightly, an echo of Persian dualism with its conflict between Ormazd and Ahriman.[1] But whereas in the Persian (and Manichaean) belief the world is the theatre of this conflict, the Christian, Gnostic and Hermetic form of the doctrine tends to represent it as entirely given over to the Adversary. 'The whole world lieth in the Evil One', says the author of the First Epistle of John; it is 'the dominion of fear and terror, the place of distress with desolation', according to a psalm from Qumran; it is 'the totality of wickedness', according to a pagan Hermetist; for the Gnostic Heracleon it is a desert peopled only by wild beasts; in the Valentinian *Gospel of Truth* it is a realm of nightmare in which 'either one flees one knows not where, or else one remains inert in pursuit of one knows not whom'.[2] To the majority of Gnostics it was unthinkable that such a world should have been created by the Supreme God: it must be the handiwork of some inferior demiurge—either, as Valentinus thought, an ignorant daemon unaware of any better possibility; or, as Marcion thought, the harsh and unintelligent God of the Old Testament; or again, as in other systems, some angel or angels in revolt against God.[3] Orthodox Chris-

---

[1] Plut., *Is. et Os.*, 46–7, 369 D ff.

[2] 1 John v. 19; M. Burrows, *Dead Sea Scrolls* (1956), p. 386; *Corp. Herm.*, vi, 4; Heracleon, fr. 20 Völker; *Evang. Veritatis*, p. 29.1 Malinine–Puech–Quispel. But such views were not universally held. With 1 John v. 19 contrast 1 Tim. iv. 4, πᾶν κτίσμα θεοῦ καλόν: with *Corp. Herm.*, vi, 4, where the cosmos is πλήρωμα τῆς κακίας, contrast xii, 15 where it is πλήρωμα τῆς ζωῆς and 'a great god, the image of a greater'. Cf. also Plutarch's protest against the view that the world is 'a place of evils' (*De tranq. an.*, 19, 477 C).

[3] The theory of an ignorant or malevolent creator—'whatever brute or blackguard made the world'—is certainly neither Greek nor Jewish, and in

tianity could not go so far: it was unwilling to throw the Book of Genesis overboard. Origen, however, maintained the substance of the Gnostic view; he attributed the creation to the action of certain 'bodiless intelligences' who became bored with contemplating God and 'turned to the inferior'.[1] To the Greek tradition an actual hypostatised Devil is wholly foreign; men like Celsus found the notion blasphemous; when Porphyry and Iamblichus speak of 'the chief of the demons' they are drawing indirectly on an Iranian source.[2] The Devil came into the West by way of late Judaism, which transformed Satan from God's agent into God's Adversary; from Judaism St Paul took him over and made him 'the god of this world', 'the prince of the power of the air'. For certain Gnostics he is 'the accursed god'; for others he is 'an angel, but in the likeness of a god'; the *Chaldaean Oracles* identified him with Hades.[3]

fact no one, I think, has suggested a plausible pre-Christian 'source' for it. So far as our present information goes, it would seem to have been first propounded in the second century after Christ. R. M. Grant, in *Gnosticism*, argues that the idea could have originated with *renegade* Jews who turned against Jehovah after his failure to protect Jerusalem from destruction in A.D. 70. This is possible, but it hardly suffices to account for the widespread adoption of this view by non-Jewish Gnostics, who do not always identify the creator-god with Jehovah (cf. W. C. van Unnik, *Vig. Chr.*, 15 (1961), pp. 65–82).

[1] Origen, *Princ.*, 2.8.3: cf. Epiphanius, *Haer.*, 64.4. For Origen 'the whole material creation is thus a result of sin, its purpose is to serve as a purgatory, and it would have been much better if there had never been any need for it' (A. H. Armstrong, *An Introduction to Ancient Philosophy* (1947), p. 173).

[2] Celsus *apud* Origen, *c. Cels.*, 6.62; Porph., *De Abst.*, 2.42 ἡ προεστῶσα αὐτῶν δύναμις: Iamb., *De myst.*, 3.30 τὸν μέγαν ἡγεμόνα τῶν δαιμόνων. Cf. Bidez–Cumont, *Les Mages hellénisés* (1938), II, pp. 275–82.

[3] 2 Cor. iv., 4; Ephes. ii. 2; Origen, *c. Cels.*, 6.27 (Ophites); Iren., *Haer.*, 1.5.2 = Völker, *Quellen*, p. 108.3 (Valentinians); H. Lewy, *Chaldaean Oracles and Theurgy* (1956), pp. 282 ff. An awareness of the Devil's true character as a projection of man's forbidden thoughts seems to be implicit in the Valentinian myth which taught that the evil spirits were created out of the remorse of Achamoth, who stands for the human soul (Clem., *Exc. ex Theod.*, 48.2; Iren., *Haer.*, 1.5.4).

When the Gnostic texts from Nag-Hammadi have all been made available, we may hope to know more about the origin and history of this wave of pessimism that swept over the West, 'this terrifying rupture between the two orders to which man belongs, the order of Reality and that of Value'.[1] But I doubt if it is to be explained entirely in terms of historical derivation. Rather than postulate with Bousset a primitive Gnostic system from which all the rest derives, I should prefer to speak, as de Faye did, of a Gnostic *tendency* which shows itself already in the first Christian century, notably in the writings of St Paul, and in the second century finds its full expression in a series of imaginative mythological structures.[2] These structures draw their imagery from many sources,

---

[1] S. Pétrement, *Le Dualisme chez Platon, etc.*, p. 157.

[2] E. de Faye, *Gnostiques et Gnosticisme* (1925), pp. 469 ff. Much confusion arises from the different senses in which different writers have used the terms 'Gnosticism' and 'Gnosis'. The systems which the Church Fathers call Gnostic appear to be variant forms of Christianity—originally, perhaps, local variants which developed at centres like Antioch and Alexandria and were later diffused by missionaries. At any rate, as Lietzmann puts it in his *Founding of the Church Universal* (Eng. trans., 1950), p. 87, 'it is impossible to draw a sharp line between Church and Gnosis'. On the other hand, some modern scholars apply the term to any system which preaches a way of escape from the world by means of a special enlightenment not available to all and not dependent on reason. In this sense the *Hermetica*, the so-called 'Mithras-liturgy', the *Chaldaean Oracles*, and even the fragments of Numenius, have all been described as 'pagan Gnosis'. And in this sense St Paul appears to be a Gnostic: cf. in particular 1 Cor. ii. 14 f., where the merely 'psychic' man is said to be incapable of gnosis, while the 'pneumatic' man judges all things and is judged by none. Some features of the Dead Sea Scrolls, taken in conjunction with Gnostic texts like the *Apocryphon of John*, suggest that the Christian Gnostics derived a good many of their ideas from heretical Jewish sects: cf. E. Peterson in *Encicl. Catt.* s.v. 'Gnosi'; G. Quispel in *The Jung Codex*, ed. Cross (1955), pp. 62–78; A. D. Nock in *J.T.S.*, N.S. 9 (1958), pp. 319 ff.; and Grant, *Gnosticism*. But nothing so far published from Qumran or Nag-Hammadi lends support to the hypothesis of a pre-Christian Gnostic *system*. For a useful summary of current views see R. M. Wilson, *The Gnostic Problem* (1958), ch. iii.

Christian and pagan, oriental and Greek, but as Burkitt saw they are very largely an hypostatisation, a dreamlike projection, of their authors' inner experience.[1] Thus the Valentinian 'Bythos', the mysterious primordial Deep where all things originally dwelt unknown, corresponds to what Augustine called the *abyssus humanae conscientiae* and to what we now call the Unconscious; and the 'barrier' (*phragmos*), which in the systems of Basileides and Valentinus cuts off the world of human experience from the world of light, corresponds to the barrier which excludes the inspirations of the Unconscious from normal consciousness.[2] Again, as Tertullian points out,[3] Valentinus saw the material world itself as a projection of the sufferings of Achamoth, the mythological counterpart of the human Ego, tormented by the longing for ultimate truth but able to produce only a bastard rationalism which has to be 'crucified away' before the Ego can be re-

[1] Cf. F. C. Burkitt, *Church and Gnosis* (1932), pp. 41 ff., from which some of my examples are taken; also A. D. Nock in *Gnomon*, 12 (1936), p. 611. I have modified Burkitt's terminology somewhat, since I am inclined to see the Gnostic teachers less as 'philosophers' in any modern sense of the word than as natural myth-makers and visionaries, men of the stamp of Swedenborg and William Blake. Some of them experienced personal visions: Valentinus saw the Logos under the form of a newborn babe, Marcus saw the Tetrad under the form of a woman (Hipp., *Haer.*, 6.42.2). Others, like Basileides, Isidore and Apelles, relied on the mediumistic utterances of inspired προφῆται: see below, p. 58, n. 2. Cf. also Porphyry's list of Gnostic 'apocalypses' (*Vit. Plot.*, 16), some of which have turned up at Nag-Hammadi.

[2] Cf. the curious prayer to be uttered after passing the *phragmos*, cited by Origen, *c. Cels.*, 6.31: βασιλέα μονότροπον, δεσμὸν ἀβλεψίας, λήθην ἀπερίσκεπτον ἀσπάζομαι: and Epiphanius, *Haer.*, 31.5: ἐπ' ἀρχῆς ὁ Αὐτοπάτωρ αὐτὸς ἐν ἑαυτῷ περιεῖχε τὰ πάντα, ὄντα ἐν ἑαυτῷ ἐν ἀγνωσίᾳ.

[3] *Adv. Valent.*, 15–20; cf. Iren., *Haer.*, 1.4.5 (Völker, *Quellen*, p. 104.25 ff.). In the Simonian myth the brothel in Tyre where the divine Helen, forgetful of her name and race, was discovered by Simon Magus (Iren., *Haer.*, 1.23.2) obviously stands for this fallen world where the soul awaits redemption.

deemed. And, finally, the splitting of God into two persons, on the one hand a remote but merciful Father, on the other a stupid and cruel Creator, seems to reflect a splitting of the individual father-image into its corresponding emotional components: the conflict of love and hate in the unconscious mind is thus symbolically resolved, and the gnawing sense of guilt is appeased.[1]

If these are the ways in which men tended to think of the world in our period, what was their view of the human condition? Clearly, in such a world what Plotinus called 'the inner man', what St Paul and the Gnostics called the 'pneumatic' or spiritual man, must have felt himself an alien and an exile; and there is abundant evidence that he did. Christians, expectant of the Second Coming, naturally thought of themselves from an early date as 'strangers and pilgrims': their instructions were 'Love not the world, neither the things that are in the world.' In the epigrammatic words of the *Letter to Diognetus*, 'They live in their own countries, but as aliens; they share all duties like citizens and suffer all disabilities like foreigners; every foreign land is their country, and every country is foreign to them.'[2] This sentiment of alienation is even stronger in the Christian Gnostics, who constituted an 'alien elect', taught an 'alien knowledge' and hoped one day to inhabit a 'new' or 'alien' earth.[3]

[1] The mother-image (for which orthodox Christianity in its older forms neglected to make any real provision) also plays an important part in several Gnostic systems. It too is split, but in a different way. On the one hand, as the heavenly Sophia (called ἡ μήτηρ, Iren., *Haer.*, 1.5.3) it is projected into the Pleroma as a divine being; on the other, as the earthly Sophia (Achamoth) it is introjected and identified with the ego.

[2] *Epist. ad Diognetum*, 5.5.

[3] Clem., *Strom.*, 4.165.3, ξένην τὴν ἐκλογὴν τοῦ κόσμου ὁ Βασιλείδης εἴληφε λέγειν: 3.2.12, τὴν ξένην, ὥς φασι, γνῶσιν εὐαγγελίζονται (of Mar-

But the sentiment is by no means confined to Christian circles: in the Platonic school it had become a commonplace.[1] Even Marcus Aurelius, whose days were spent in administering an empire, could express at times the desolate sense of not belonging: 'All the life of man's body is a stream that flows, all the life of his mind, dream and delirium; his existence a warfare and a sojourn in a strange land; his after-fame, oblivion.' He fought against the exclusive dominion of such thoughts with all the strength of his Stoic religion, reminding himself that his existence was part and parcel of the great Unity. But they were the thoughts of his time, and he could not escape them: he could only ask, 'How long?'[2]

Such reflections inevitably raised the question, 'What are we here for?' (ἐπὶ τί γεγόναμεν;). It is an old question. Empedocles asked it and offered an answer; Plato in the *Theaetetus* affirmed that it was the proper subject of philosophical enquiry.[3] But it is not in fact a question which happy men readily ask themselves; a happy life appears to be its own justification. It was only under the Empire

cionites); Plot., II, ix, 11.11, ἡ γῆ αὐτοῖς ἡ ξένη λεγομένη: II, ix, 5.24, καινὴν ... γῆν (cf. C. A. Baynes, *Coptic Gnostic Treatise* (1933), p. 136). Celsus attributed a like belief to the Christians (Origen, *c. Cels.*, 7.28): cf. Revelation, xxi. 1. The Sethian sect actually called themselves 'Strangers' (ἀλλογενεῖς) and gave the same name to Seth, the central figure in their mythology; an unpublished work found at Nag-Hammadi is entitled *Allogenes Hypsistos*. Compare Tolstoi's 'feeling of dread that made me seem like an orphan and isolated in the midst of all these things that were so foreign' (*My Confession*).

[1] [Plato], *Axiochus*, 365 B τὸ κοινὸν δὴ τοῦτο καὶ πρὸς ἁπάντων θρυλούμενον, παρεπιδημία τίς ἐστιν ὁ βίος.

[2] M. Ant., 2.17 (cf. also 12.1.2, ξένος ὢν τῆς πατρίδος); 7.9; 6.46 μέχρι τίνος οὖν; The evolution of the related notion of ἀναχώρησις has been examined by Festugière, *Personal Religion*, ch. iv.

[3] Plato, *Theaet.*, 174 B. On the earlier history of the question see Dodds, *Greeks*, ch. v.

that both philosophers and other men began to treat it as a major problem.[1] They provided a wide variety of answers, which Festugière has classified,[2] starting from the doxography given by Iamblichus in his essay *On the Soul*. He divides them into two main groups, optimistic and pessimistic. For those who held fast to the old faith in the divinity of the cosmos the *Timaeus* offered an easy answer: without humanity the perfection of the world would be incomplete.[3] In other terms, we are here, as a second-century Platonist put it, 'for the revelation of divine life'[4]—human existence is part of the self-realisation of God. Others, starting from the Platonic saying that 'all life cares for the lifeless everywhere', saw man as God's administrator and earthly existence as a form of service (*leitourgia*). This could be understood in an optimistic or a pessimistic sense. 'Service to life', Celsus calls it; Marcus Aurelius, more bitterly, 'service to the flesh'; the Indian sages of Bardesanes thought of it as 'a compulsory service to nature' which they endured reluctantly.[5] Such service can be perilous to the soul, which Plotinus touchingly compares to the steersman who unthinkingly

[1] Examples were collected by Norden, *Agnostos Theos* (1913), pp. 101–9. Whether we should follow him in tracing them all back to a 'model' composed by Poseidonius seems to me very doubtful: for most of the authors concerned the question is much more than a rhetorical τόπος. A recent addition to the collection is *Evang. Veritatis*, p. 22.4 ff. Malinine–Puech–Quispel.

[2] Festugière, *Révélation*, III, ch. ii, from which much of the material in this paragraph and the next is taken.

[3] Plato, *Tim.*, 41 B–C.

[4] εἰς θείας ζωῆς ἐπίδειξιν, attributed by Iamblichus, *apud* Stob., 1.379.1, to the school of Taurus. Cf. Plot. IV, viii, 5.29–37.

[5] Plato, *Phdr.*, 246 B; Celsus *apud* Origen, *c. Cels.*, 8.53; M. Ant., 6.28; Bardesanes *apud* Porph., *De abst.*, 4.18, p. 258.14 Nauck. For Synesius it is service to the cosmos (*De prov.*, P.G. 66, 1229 A) or to Nature (*De insomn.*, 1296 B). The optimistic version *may* derive from Poseidonius (*apud* Clem., *Strom.*, 2.129: cf. A. D. Nock in *J.R.S.*, 49 (1959), 12).

risks his life in his determination to save his ship.[1] He
holds, however, that on balance the soul may gain from
its experience of evil. For Proclus such experience is a
necessary part of our education; and in some Christian
Platonists we find a related conception of the world as a
'school for souls'.[2]

But to the more radical dualists explanations of this
kind appeared insufficient. If man is an alien wanderer on
the face of the earth, his presence here can only be due to
a Fall, a loss of his wings as in the *Phaedrus* myth. It is, as
Iamblichus put it, 'unnatural'.[3] On this view birth is
frankly a misfortune: wise men do not celebrate their
birthdays.[4] Man's fallen state could be accounted for in
either of two ways: as the punishment for an earlier sin
committed in Heaven, or as the result of a false choice
made by the soul itself. The notion of incarnation as
punishment seems to be in origin Pythagorean and Orphic: it appears in the old Pythagorean catechism; Aristotle ascribed it to 'the exponents of mysteries', Crantor
more vaguely to 'many of the wise'.[5] From such a source,

[1] Plot., IV, iii, 17.21 ff. Cf. Numenius fr. 20 Leemans (*apud* Eus., *Praep.
Ev.*, 11. 17), where the Demiurge or world-soul 'through caring for Matter
becomes neglectful of himself; reaching out towards Matter, he enters into
contact with the sensible, tends it, and elevates it to his own character'; and
Proclus *In Alc.*, p. 32.11 ff. Creuzer.

[2] Plot. IV, iii, 7.11–17; Proclus, *Dec. dub.*, 38.7 Boese; Basil, *H. in Hex.*,
1.5, the world as διδασκαλεῖον καὶ παιδευτήριον τῶν ἀνθρωπίνων ψυχῶν.

[3] Iamb., *Protrept.*, 60.10 ff. (certainly not from Aristotle: see I. Düring,
Aristotle's Protrepticus (1961), p. 257).

[4] Origen, *In Levit.*, hom. viii, 3, 'sancti non solum non agunt festivitatem
in die natali suo, sed in spiritu sancto repleti exsecrantur hunc diem'. Plotinus
similarly refused to celebrate his birthday, Porph., *Vit. Plot.*, 2.37 ff.

[5] Iamb., *Vit. Pyth.*, 85 (=*Vorsokr.*, 58 C 4); Aristotle, *Protrept.*, fr. 106
Düring (=fr. 60 Rose³); Crantor *apud* Plut. (?) *Cons. ad Apoll.*, 27, 115 B.
It was from the philosophers, according to Clement, that the Marcionites
learned this 'impious' doctrine (*Strom.*, 3.3).

combined with the Jewish belief in fallen angels, it was taken over by Christian or semi-Christian Gnostics (Valentinus, Marcion, Bardesanes, Mani); also, it would seem, by Origen; and likewise by the pagan Hermetist who composed the *Kore Kosmou*. According to the last-named the offence of the souls was disobedience inspired by an impertinent self-assertion (*tolma*).[1] Slightly less mythological is the alternative form of the doctrine, in which the descent is deliberately chosen by the soul and constitutes its offence. This appears in Numenius, in the Hermetic *Poimandres*, and sometimes in Plotinus. The soul's motive is described as love for Nature or Matter, or more subtly as narcissism—she falls in love with her own image reflected upon the material world—or again as ambition or *tolma*.[2] Where the term *tolma* appears it points to a Pythagorean source, for we know that *tolma* was a Pythagorean name for the Dyad, the principle of strife opposed to the One.[3] When Augustine tells us that '*audacia* separates the soul from God',[4] his *audacia* is a translation of *tolma*.

Plotinus' treatment of the question deserves a word to itself, since it has not, I fancy, been fully understood. He

---

[1] *Kore Kosmou*, 24 (*Corp. Herm.*, vol. IV, 8 Nock–Festugière). As to Origen, see above, p. 17, n. 1.

[2] Love for ὕλη or φύσις, Numenius, fr. 20 Leemans, *Poim.* (*Corp. Herm.*, i) 14; narcissism, Plot., IV, iii, 12.1, *Poim., ibid.*; ambition to create or govern, Dio Chrys., *Borysth.*, 55, Plot. v, i, 1.3 (τόλμα), *Poim.*, 13. τόλμα also in later Neoplatonists, e.g. Hierocles, 148.19 ff., Proclus, *Mal. subst.*, 12.13 Boese.

[3] Plut., *Is. et Os.*, 381 F; Anatolius *apud* [Iamb.], *Theol. Arithm.*, p. 7.19 de Falco; Olympiodorus, *In Alc.*, 48.17 Cr. Cf. Proclus, *In Alc.*, 132.13 Cr. τὴν πρόοδον ταύτην 'τόλμαν' ἀποκαλεῖ τὸν Πυθαγόρειον τρόπον. Lydus, *De mens.*, 2.7, attributes this use of τόλμα to 'the school of Pherecydes': he had perhaps found the term in a Pythagorean 'Pherecydes' forgery.

[4] Augustine, *De moribus*, 1.20: cf. *De mus.*, 6.40; *Civ. Dei*, 22.24, on the *audacia* of Adam; and W. Theiler, *Porphyrios und Augustin* (1933), pp. 27–30.

has been accused of inconsistent and muddled thinking on this matter: not quite fairly, for, as he pointed out, the inconsistency was there in the writings of his master Plato.[1] Viewed historically, the problem was, and is, to reconcile the cosmology of the *Timaeus* with the psychology of the *Phaedo* and the *Phaedrus*. In one early essay Plotinus made a first attempt, not very successful, at reconciling them.[2] But in his earlier work generally he tends to accept the pessimistic assumption, inherited from Numenius, that the individual soul has descended by a deliberate act of choice, wishing wilfully 'to govern a part of the world by herself' or 'to be her own master'.[3] In three successive essays he uses the Pythagorean *tolma*-language in this connection.[4] A change comes when he breaks finally with Gnosticism. In the essay *Against the Gnostics* it is his opponents who think that the soul created the world 'out of arrogance and *tolma*'.[5] Henceforth the *tolma*-language is

[1] Plot., IV, viii, 1. On Plotinus' inconsistency see, e.g. Inge, *Phil. of Plotinus*[3] (1929), I, p. 259; Bréhier, *La Philosophie de Plotin* (1928), pp. 64–8; Festugière, *Révélation*, III, 95 f.; and most recently C. Tresmontant, *Métaphysique du Christianisme* (1962), pp. 319–44. None of these writers considers the possibility of a development in Plotinus' thought on this matter. Such a development is, however, recognised, and brought into relation with the controversy against the Gnostics, by J. Guitton, *Le Temps et l'éternité chez Plotin et Saint Augustin*[3] (1959), pp. 71–86.

[2] IV, viii, 5. Plotinus seems to be groping here towards something like his later view, but his words are obscure (and are further obscured by textual corruption at a critical point, lines 16 ff.). This essay is 'chron., 6', i.e. the sixth in Porphyry's chronological ordering of the 54 essays.

[3] IV, vii (chron., 2), 13.11; V, i (chron., 10), 1.5. Cf. also IV, viii (chron., 6), 4.10–28.

[4] VI, ix (chron., 9), 5.29 Br., the separation of Nous from the One is an act of τόλμα; V, i (chron., 10), 1.4, τόλμα the beginning of evil for the soul; V, ii (chron., 11), 2.5, the vegetative part of the soul is τὸ τολμηρότατον καὶ ἀφρονέστατον.

[5] II, ix (chron., 23), 11.21. For another instance in this essay of the rejection of a Numenian and Gnostic view which Plotinus had himself tentatively adopted earlier see *Les Sources de Plotin*, pp. 19 f. The importance of the break

dropped from his own teaching, and the descent even of the individual soul is no longer viewed as a sin. In IV, iii, 13 we have his mature view on the question: there the souls descend 'neither deliberately nor at God's command' but *instinctively* in obedience to an inner 'instruction' (*prothesmia*), as a cow grows horns; the necessity is biological.[1] Here Plotinus has at last emancipated himself from Numenian influence. And final confirmation is furnished by one of his latest writings, the essay on *The Person and the Organism*, where we are told that the illumination of body by soul is no more a sin than casting a shadow.[2] Whatever his earlier doubts, Plotinus emerges in the end as the upholder of Hellenic rationalism.

I have now described, as best I could in short compass, what seem to be the characteristic attitudes of the time towards the world and man's place in it. It remains to ask what evidence we have of their effects on human behaviour. Clearly, such attitudes could not encourage men 'to utilize or improve the external world', and in fact the third century has little effort to show in this direction—until we come down to the reforms of Diocletian, which were based on the new theocratic concept of the Emperor

with Gnosticism as a critical point in the development of Plotinus' thought is emphasised in the discussion reported further on in the same volume, pp. 182–90. Recognition of this seems to open the way to a 'genetic' study of his philosophy on sounder lines than those followed in F. H. Heinemann's unlucky book.

[1] IV, iii (chron., 27), 13. The thought is developed in a wider context in the continuation of this essay, at IV, iv (chron., 28), 11.

[2] I, i (chron., 53), 12.24. Cf. also I, viii (chron. 51), where the association of soul and body is treated as natural: the soul's 'weakness' is not inherent in it but is due to the presence of Matter (ch. 14), which is itself a necessary consequence of the dynamic expansion from the One (ch. 7). The same feeling inspires I, iv (chron., 46), 16.20 ff., where the wise man is said to care for his body as the musician for his lyre.

as God's representative on earth. But we must not simply equate other-worldliness with indifference. We may feel that a Marcus Aurelius or a Plotinus cared more for self-perfection than for life; but we should remember that Marcus worked harder for human welfare than most men have done, and that Plotinus took time off from contemplating the One to make his house into an orphanage and act as trustee for its inmates, 'hearing them their recitations' and 'examining the accounts of their property and checking their accuracy'.[1] On the other side, there is ample testimony to the philanthropic activity of the Christian churches: to quote a single example, in the middle of the third century the community at Rome was supporting over 1500 'widows and poor persons'.[2] And they did not confine their help to fellow-Christians: 'These godless Galilaeans', said Julian crossly, 'feed not only their own poor but others, while we neglect our own.'[3] I shall return to this point in ch. IV.

A more positive effect which we might expect to find, and do find, is an *introjection* of the hostile feeling: resent-

[1] Porph., *Vit. Plot.*, 9. It is clear nevertheless that for Plotinus the life of action is a poor second-best, in principle unworthy of a contemplative (VI, ix, 7.26); the true philosopher will resign all public offices (I, iv, 14.20), as Plotinus's pupil Rogatianus did (*Vit. Plot.*, 7.35). If the abortive project for a 'Platonopolis' (*ibid.*, 12) had come to fruition, it would surely have been more like a Christian monastery than like Plato's Ideal State. Marcus was more realistic: 'Do not hope for Plato's Utopia; be content if you can make the smallest step forward, and reflect that the result even of this is no trifle' (9.29).

[2] Eus., *Hist. Eccl.*, 6.43.11. The widows' lot would be the harder since re-marriage was severely discountenanced. Much further evidence will be found in Harnack, *Mission*, II, ch. iv.

[3] Julian, *Epist.*, 84a Bidez–Cumont, 430 d. Cf. J. Kabiersch, *Unters. zum Begriff der Philanthropie bei dem Kaiser Julian*, and the reviews by M. J. Boyd (*C.R.*, 76 (1962), pp. 167 f.) and R. Browning (*J.H.S.*, 82 (1962), p. 192). An earlier (and equally reluctant) pagan witness to Christian mutual help is Lucian, *Peregr.*, 13. See also below, p. 136–8.

ment against the world becomes, or carries with it, resentment against the ego—what Seneca called 'displicentia sui'.[1] This can find vent in either of two main ways: in the purely mental torment inflicted by a too tender conscience—in Freud's language, by a nagging Super-ego— or else in physical acts of self-punishment, in extreme cases even self-mutilation or suicide. Self-reproach is frequent in Christian writers of all periods: naturally so, since their creed makes moral demands which are incapable of complete fulfilment. Among pagans it is comparatively rare. Self-examination is recommended in the Pythagorean *Golden Verses*: do not go to sleep until you have considered all that you did or failed to do in the course of the day; censure yourself for the bad deeds and rejoice in the good ones. The advice was quoted with approval by Epictetus, and practised by Seneca.[2] In our period the most striking examples of moral self-reproach are to be found where they seem least necessary, in Marcus Aurelius. Resentment against the world being for him the worst impiety, he turns it inward upon himself. Already in a letter to Fronto, written at the age of 25, he is angry about his own failure to achieve the philosophic life: 'I do penance,' he says, 'I am cross with myself, I am sad and discontented, I feel starved.'[3] The same feelings

[1] Sen., *De tranq.*, 2.10. His analysis of self-dissatisfaction has a very modern ring, and deserves a closer study than I can give it here.

[2] *Carm. aur.*, 40–4, quoted by Epictetus, 3.10.2; cf. Sen., *De ira*, 3.36.3 ff. *Confession* of sin, auricular or public, is foreign to the Greek tradition, but is not peculiar to Christianity: cf. R. Pettazzoni, *La confessione dei peccati* (1929– 36), and 'Confessions of Sins and the Classics', in *Harv. Theol. Rev.*, 30 (1937), pp. 1 ff.

[3] Fronto, *Epist.* vol. 1, p. 216 Loeb. Cf. Georg Misch's perceptive chapter on Marcus in his *History of Autobiography in Antiquity* (Eng. trans., 1950), vol. II.

haunt him as Emperor: he has fallen short of his ideals and missed the good life; his existence has scarred and soiled him; he longs to be other than he is, to 'begin at last to be a human being' before he dies. 'It is hard', he says, 'for a man to endure himself.'[1]

Other men in this time (and Marcus himself in other moods) were enabled to endure themselves by making a sharp dichotomy between the self and the body, and diverting their resentment on to the latter. That dichotomy comes, of course, from classical Greece[2]—the most far-reaching, and perhaps the most questionable, of all her gifts to human culture. But in our period it was put to strange uses. Pagans and Christians (though not all pagans or all Christians) vied with each other in heaping abuse on the body; it was 'clay and gore', 'a filthy bag of excrement and urine'; man is plunged in it as in a bath of dirty water. Plotinus appeared ashamed of having a body at all; St Anthony blushed every time he had to eat or satisfy any other bodily function.[3] Because the body's life was the soul's death, salvation lay in mortifying it; as

---

[1] M. Ant., 8.1.1; 10.8, 1–2; 11.18.5; 5.10.1. With these passages it is tempting to link the dream dreamt by Marcus before he became Emperor, in which he seemed to have hands and arms of ivory but could use them like human arms (Dio Cass., 71.36.1). Taken together, they suggest that Marcus experienced in a severe form what modern psychologists call a 'crisis of identity'. But while so much self-reproach may seem to us morbid, there is no hint in Marcus of a view like Tertullian's that 'the torturing of the soul' is a sacrifice pleasing to God (*De esu carn.*, 8).

[2] I have discussed the origins of the idea in *Greeks*, ch. v.

[3] M. Ant., 3.3; Arnobius, 2.37; M. Ant., 8.24; Porph., *Vit. Plot.*, 1; Athanasius, *Vit. Ant.*, 45, 909 A. Cf. also *Regula Pachomii*, 30, which forbids monks to watch each other eating; and Jerome, *Epist.*, 107.11, girls should never take baths lest they should see their own bodies naked. For a different attitude to the body see Plut., *Sto. rep.*, 21, 1044 B ff.; Clem., *Strom.*, 4.4. 17 f., 4.26.163–5; Origen, *c. Cels.*, 3.42, 'In itself bodily nature is not involved in evil'.

a Desert Father expressed it, 'I am killing it because it is killing me'.[1] The psychophysical unity was split in two not only in theory but in practice; one half found its satisfaction in tormenting the other.

This sort of asceticism takes us a long way from the old Greek ἄσκησις, a word which in Plato and Aristotle means simply 'training'. Antecedents of a sort can be discovered for this or that ascetic practice in earlier Greek teaching,[2] but the origin of the movement as a whole remains obscure. We have descriptions of a number of ascetic communities which appear to have sprung up independently in different parts of the eastern Mediter-

---

[1] *Heraclidis Paradeisos*, 1. That this life is the death of the soul is an old thought, going back to Heraclitus and Empedocles, but in our period it is associated with a new intensity of feeling. The body is 'the dark gaol, the living death, the corpse revealed, the tomb that we carry about with us' (*Corp. Herm.*, vii, 2). The recently published *Gospel of Thomas* stresses the need for total alienation from it: 'Woe to the flesh that hangs upon the soul! Woe to the soul that hangs upon the flesh!' (110). The doctrine of the resurrection of the body may have had some effect in deterring Christians from extreme denigration of the body (cf. Tert., *De res. carn.*, 4 f.); but the effect did not reach very far. At *De anima*, 53, after quoting St Paul's description of the body as 'the temple of God', Tertullian immediately goes on to say that it obstructs, obscures and sullies the soul. Daniélou's claim that Christian asceticism in the third and fourth centuries 'was not based on contempt for the body, as pagan asceticism was' (*Origen*, Eng. trans., 1955, p. 12), appears to me to be much too sweeping. Not all pagan ascetics vilified the body: Porphyry tells us that the sinner should blame not his body but his soul (*Ad Marc.*, 29). For the attitude of the Desert Fathers, on the other hand, cf. e.g. Athan., *Vit. Ant.*, 22 f.; *Apophth. Patrum*, 10.17; and the evidence assembled by O. Zöckler in his *Askese und Mönchtum*, I, 236–68. This body-hatred should be distinguished from the world-wide practice of ἄσκησις (*a*) as a means to ritual purity (usually temporary); (*b*) as a means of strengthening one's *mana* (cf. H. J. Rose, *Cl. Phil.*, 20 (1925), pp. 238 ff.); (*c*) as an exercise to fortify the will. (The last is typically Pythagorean: cf. Diod., 10.5.2; Diog. Laert., 8.13; Iamb., *Vit. Pyth.*, 187; Epict., 3.12.17.)

[2] Cf. J. Leipoldt, 'Griech. Philosophie und frühchristliche Askese', *Verh. Sächs. Akad.*, Phil.-hist. Kl., 106. iv (1961). Much material on ἄσκησις is also collected in L. Bieler's Θεῖος Ἀνήρ (1935–6), I, pp. 60–73.

ranean shortly before the time of Christ: Essenes in
Palestine, Therapeutae round Lake Mareotis, the Egyptian contemplatives described by Chaeremon, and Neo-
pythagoreans in Rome. Unfortunately, apart from the
Qumran documents, none of these speak to us with their
own voice; we have only second-hand descriptions, in
which it is difficult to distinguish historical fact from the
literary presentation of an ideal. How far did any of
these communities influence Christian asceticism? I know
of no decisive answer. Holl and Reitzenstein[1] showed that
Athanasius' *Life of St Anthony* owed something to a pagan
Life of Pythagoras; this is not altogether surprising, since
hagiography was a literary genre common to Christians
and pagans—we have pagan specimens in Philostratus'
life of Apollonius, Marinus' life of Proclus, and Eunapius'
lives of Neoplatonic philosophers. But, as Festugière has
pointed out,[2] it does not at all follow that Christian
ascetic *practice* was derived from pagan models. There is
some rather slight evidence for the existence of 'pagan
hermits' before the Christian eremitic movement, but it
would be rash to conclude that their example influenced
the Desert Fathers; we can only say that the same psychological impulses may have been at work in both. If there
was a model, it was probably Jewish rather than pagan.[3]

[1] K. Holl, *Gesammelte Aufsätze*, II, 249 ff.; R. Reitzenstein, *Sitzb. Heid.*
1914, Abt. viii. (Reitzenstein as usual pressed his point a good deal further
than the evidence strictly justifies: see H. Dörries, *Nachr. Gött.* 1949, p. 401.)

[2] *R.E.G.*, 50 (1937), p. 478.

[3] The only 'pagan hermit' known to us by name seems to be Sostratus, who
lived in the open on Mount Parnassus and is said to have supported life entirely
on milk (Lucian, *Demonax*, 1; Plut., Q. *Symp.*, 4.1.1), but there is no evidence
that his motive was religious (he engaged in practical activities like fighting
bandits and making roads). Plutarch's holy man who lived in the Arabian
desert and ate once a month (*Def. or.*, 421 A) is fictional. Jerome, however,

The major difference between pagan and Christian asceticism can best be appreciated by looking at the *Sentences of Sextus*, a collection of religious and moral aphorisms which survives both in the form given to it by a Christian redactor about the end of the second century and also in several older pagan versions.[1] The asceticism of the pagan aphorisms is moderate, not to say banal: self-control is the foundation of piety; we should eat only when hungry, sleep only when we must, avoid getting drunk, and have sex relations only for child-getting.[2] But on the last point the Christian redactor takes a much grimmer view: marriage, if ventured on at all, should be 'a competition in continence', and self-castration is preferable to impurity.[3] Such opinions were widely held, and sometimes acted on, by Christian and Gnostic rigorists. Both Galen and Origen testify that many contemporary Christians abstained from sex relations throughout their lives; virginity was 'the supreme and crowning achievement'; the widely read *Acts of Paul and Thecla* taught that only virgins will be resurrected; the Marcionites are said to have refused the sacraments to

knows of Pythagoreans who 'in solitudine et desertis locis habitare consueverunt' (*Adv. Jovinian.*, 2.9), and Porphyry confirms him (*De abst.*, 1.36). The Jewish tradition of eremitism is much older and stronger (Elijah, John the Baptist, the Therapeutae). Josephus spent three years in the wilderness with one Bannus who 'wore only such clothing as trees provided, feeding on such things as grew of themselves, and using frequent ablutions of cold water, by day and night, for purity's sake' (*Vita*, 2).

[1] The priority of the pagan versions—the χρειῶν συναγωγή of Clitarchus, the *Pythagorean Sentences*, and the maxims used by Porphyry in the *Ad Marcellam*—has been firmly established by H. Chadwick in his admirable edition of Sextus (1959).

[2] Clit., 13 (=Sext., 86ᵃ); 97; 87; 116; 70 (cf. Sext., 232 and Clem., *Strom.*, 3.24).

[3] Sextus, 239, cf. 230ᵃᵇ; 13, cf. 273.

married persons,[1] as for adultery, in the early Church it
was commonly classed with murder and apostasy as an
unforgivable sin.[2] Justin Martyr quotes with approval a
case of attempted self-castration, and Origen (if we can
believe Eusebius) castrated himself while little more than
a boy. At a later date such acts were not infrequent
among the Desert Fathers; in the fourth century it was
found necessary to prohibit them by canon law.[3] Of continuous physical self-torture the lives of the Desert
Fathers provide numerous and repulsive examples:
several live for years on top of pillars, another immures
himself in a packing-case where he cannot stand upright,
others remain perpetually in a standing position; others
again load themselves with heavy chains (the skeleton of
one of these has been found in Egypt, chains and all);
others pride themselves on such feats of endurance as
total abstinence from food throughout Lent—I need not
prolong the catalogue.[4]

[1] Galen, fragment from the Arabic in Walzer's *Galen*, p. 15; Origen, *c. Cels.*,
7.48; Methodius, *Symp.*, 1, 2; *Acta Pauli et Theclae*, 12; Tert., *Adv. Marc.*, 1.29.
The *Gospel of the Egyptians* taught that Christ came 'to destroy the works of the
female', i.e. to put an end to sexual reproduction (Clem., *Strom.*, 3.9.63). And
the same view appears in a reputedly 'apostolic' writing, *2 Clem.*, 12.

[2] For the evidence see Kirk, *Vision*, pp. 222–9. The intensity of the malice
felt by the chaste against the unchaste may be seen in the second-century
Apocalypse of Peter, where the post-mortem tortures to be inflicted on adul-
terers, fornicators and homosexuals are described in detail and with relish.

[3] Justin, *Apol. i*, 29; Eus., *Hist. Eccl.*, 6.8; Epiphanius, *De fide*, 13; *Apostolic
Canons*, 23. Cf. Chadwick, *The Sentences of Sextus*, pp. 110–12. The opinion
that castration is preferable to impurity is not, however, exclusively Christian:
as Professor Chadwick points out to me, it appears already in Philo, *Quod det.
pot.*, 176. In his discussion of Matthew xix. 12 Origen quoted the views of
Philo and Sextus, but only to condemn them (*Comm. in Matt.* 15.3).—It seems
likely that the impulse of self-aggression was also a determining factor in some
cases of voluntary martyrdom by self-denunciation: see below, p. 135, n. 4.

[4] Cf. A.-J. Festugière, *Antioche païenne et chrétienne* (1959), chs. ix and xii;
Les Moines d'Orient, I. Culture ou Sainteté (1961), ch. iii. For the chained skeleton

Where did all this madness come from? Again I do not
know. Despite Reitzenstein, and more recently Leipoldt,[1]
I cannot believe that it had substantial roots in Hellenic
tradition. For the sort of ideas and practices described in
the last paragraph, the Greek parallels known to me are
both inadequate and poorly authenticated;[2] they were

see C. Butler, *Lausiac History of Palladius* (1898), II, p. 215. In seeking to explain
such behaviour we must of course allow for the influence of other motives than
the need for self-punishment. In many cases there is a strong element of com-
petitive display (cf. A.-J. Festugière in *Hermes*, 73 (1955), pp. 272–7): Macarius
of Alexandria outdoes all the other monks in fasting, and thereby arouses their
angry jealousy (*Hist. Laus.*, 18, p. 52.1 ff. Butler); Sarapion brags, 'I am deader
than you' (ἐγὼ σοῦ νεκρότερός εἰμι, ibid., 37, p. 115.17). Jerome's bitter
description of the 'sovereign arrogance' of his fellow-hermits is illuminating,
Epist. 17. Among the reported motives for the retreat to the desert, a sense of
guilt is the most frequent but by no means the only one: Narcissus, the
earliest recorded Christian hermit (second century) is actuated by disgust at
being slandered (Eus., *Hist. Eccl.*, 6.9.4–6); others are said to have been influenced by family quarrels (*Hist. Mon.*, 24.1; Callinicus, *Vit. Hypatii*, 1); or
by simple distaste for humanity (*Apophth. Patrum*, 7.33; 11.5).

[1] Reitzenstein, *Hell. Wund.*, pp. 142 ff.; J. Leipoldt, *op. cit.* (see p. 30,
n. 2), and Dihle's review in *Gnomon*, 34 (1962), pp. 453 ff. For a careful
analysis and criticism of Reitzenstein's theory see Kirk, *Vision*, pp. 491–503.

[2] The main source is Philostratus' fictional biography of Apollonius of
Tyana. It is poor evidence, being an idealised portrait of the perfect θεῖος ἀνήρ,
not a description of an actual way of life. But the asceticism Philostratus attri-
butes to his hero is by contemporary Christian standards quite moderate.
Apollonius practises sexual abstinence (1.13), and of course vegetarianism; he
takes the Pythagorean vow of silence (1.14: this was admired by Eusebius,
Adv. Hieroclem, p. 381 Kayser, and is said to have been imitated by the Gnostic
Basileides, *Hist. Eccl.*, 4.7.11); he disapproves of hot baths (1.16), as do many
Christians, even the moderate Clement (*Paid.*, 3.46–8). But there is no suggestion of self-torture or systematic 'warfare' against the body. Clement, who
speaks with approval of Pythagorean continence, points out that it is not inspired by any hatred of life, since it authorises sex relations for the purpose of
child-getting (*Strom.*, 3.24). And even the fanatical late Neoplatonist Theose-
bius, ὁ πάντων σωφρονέστατος, who presented his wife with a chastity-belt and
told her to wear it or get out, did not do so until all hope of children had faded
(Damascius, *Vit. Isidori*, 59), whereas praise of the 'mariage blanc' is a constantly recurrent theme in the popular Christian apocrypha. When Tertullian
(*Praescr. haer.*, 40) tells us that the Devil too has his virgins and *continentes* he is
probably thinking of the ritual requirements of certain pagan cults—taboo
rather than asceticism.

condemned by pagan moralists like Plutarch and Epictetus, and Christians of Hellenic culture like Clement of
Alexandria resisted them firmly.[1] They have no roots in
the Old Testament; nor any, I think (apart from one passage of disputed meaning[2]) in the teachings ascribed to
the Founder of Christianity. For the fantastic value attached to virginity St Paul would appear to be mainly
responsible, though 1 Corinthians vii suggests that his
opinions were less extreme than those of the community
he was addressing. It was at any rate from his writings
that the rigorists culled the texts to justify their psychological obsession. Saner men took the view that 'the
Church, like Noah's ark, must find room for the unclean
as well as the clean animals';[3] but a strong injection
of fanatical rigorism had been absorbed into the Church's
system. It lingered there like a slow poison, and (if an
outsider can judge) has not yet been expelled from it.

That, however, is another story. What I have tried to
show in this chapter is that contempt for the human condition and hatred of the body was a disease endemic in the
entire culture of the period; that while its more extreme
manifestations are mainly Christian or Gnostic, its
symptoms show themselves in a milder form in pagans of
purely Hellenic education; and that this disease found expression in a wide variety of myths and fantasies, some

---

[1] Plut., *Sto. rep.*, 21, 1044 B ff.; *Q. Conv.*, 7.7, 710 B ff.; *Tuend. san.*, 17,
131 B; Epict., 3.12.1, τὰς ἀσκήσεις οὐ δεῖ διὰ τῶν παρὰ φύσιν καὶ παραδόξων
ποιεῖσθαι. Cf. Clement's defence of marriage, *Strom.*, 3.86; of meat-eating,
Paed., 2.9.2; of wine-drinking, *Paed.*, 2.32; of the possession of riches, *Paed.*,
3.34–6.
[2] Matt. xix. 12. Cf. H. von Campenhausen, 'Die Askese im Urchristen-
tum', in his *Tradition und Leben* (1960), pp. 114–56.
[3] Anon., *Ad Novatianum*, 2 (Cyprian, *C.S.E.L.*, III, iii, 55).

drawn from Greek, others from oriental originals (often with a changed meaning or a changed emphasis), while others again are apparently new. I incline to see the whole development less as an infection from an extraneous source than as an endogenous neurosis, an index of intense and widespread guilt-feelings. The material distresses of the third century certainly encouraged it, but they did not occasion it, since its beginnings, as we have seen, lie further back.

CHAPTER II

MAN AND THE DAEMONIC WORLD

We are lived by Powers we pretend to understand.

IN chapter I I described the progressive devaluation of the cosmos in the early Christian centuries (in other words, the progressive withdrawal of divinity from the material world), and the corresponding devaluation of ordinary human experience. In the next two I shall describe some *extra*-ordinary experiences of which the record has survived from the second and third centuries. For the present chapter I shall take as my text that passage in the *Symposium* where Plato defines the daemonic. 'Everything that is daemonic', says Diotima to Socrates, 'is intermediate between God and mortal. Interpreting and conveying the wishes of men to gods and the will of gods to men, it stands between the two and fills the gap. . . . God has no contact with man; only through the daemonic is there intercourse and conversation between men and gods, whether in the waking state or during sleep. And the man who is expert in such intercourse is a daemonic man, compared with whom the experts in arts or handicrafts are but journeymen.'[1] This precise definition of the vague terms 'daemon' and 'daemonios' was something of a novelty in Plato's day, but in the second cen-

[1] Plato, *Symp.*, 202 D 13–203 A 6.

tury after Christ it was the expression of a truism. Virtually every one, pagan, Jewish, Christian or Gnostic, believed in the existence of these beings and in their function as mediators, whether he called them daemons or angels or aions or simply 'spirits' (πνεύματα). In the eyes of many pious pagans even the gods of Greek mythology were by this time no more than mediating daemons, satraps of an invisible supramundane King.[1] And the 'daemonic man', who knew how to establish contact with them, was correspondingly esteemed.

I shall begin with dreamers. 'It is to dreams,' says Tertullian, 'that the majority of mankind owe their knowledge of God'[2]—a sentiment with which E. B. Tylor would have agreed. Certainly, of all modes of contact with the supernatural, dreaming is, and was in antiquity, the most widely practised. As Synesius remarked, it is the one mode of divination which is equally open to the slave and the millionaire, since it costs nothing and requires no apparatus; and no tyrant can forbid it unless he forbids his subjects to sleep.[3] This is no doubt one reason

---

[1] Cf. e.g. [Ar.], *De mundo*, 6; Aristides, *Orat.*, 43.18 Keil; Celsus *apud* Origen, *c. Cels.*, 7.68; see also below, pp. 117 f. Plutarch, *Def. orac.*, 13, 417 A, attributes the operation of oracles to subordinate daemons. A related tendency is shown by the Roman imperial coinage, where the images of mythological gods are increasingly replaced by edifying abstractions (F. Gnecchi, *Monete Romane*[3] (1907), pp. 290–9). The importance of the trend towards monotheism, at least among the educated classes, has recently been emphasised and illustrated by M. P. Nilsson, *Harv. Theol. Rev.*, 56(1963), pp. 101 ff. But pagans as well as Christians needed an accessible mediator between themselves and the High God; and paganism as well as Christianity provided such figures.

[2] Tert., *De anima*, 47.2. He holds, however, that many dreams are sent by evil demons; and this was the general opinion of the Apologists(Justin, *Apol.* i, 14; Tatian, *Orat.*, 18; Athenag., *Leg.*, 27).

[3] Synesius, *De insomniis*, 8. If this essay belongs, as it seems to do, to Synesius' pagan period, the mention of tyrannical prohibitions perhaps alludes to the edicts of Christian emperors against pagan modes of divination.

why dreaming, alone among pagan divinatory practices, was tolerated by the Christian Church. But the divinatory dream had also firm scriptural authority: had not St Peter himself quoted the saying of the prophet Joel, 'Your old men shall dream dreams, your young men shall see visions'?[1] As for the classical Greek tradition of the 'divine' or 'oracular' dream, I will not repeat what can be found in my book, *The Greeks and the Irrational*. ~~I will only remark in passing that I am less sure now than I was when I wrote it that the 'divine' dreams so often recorded in antiquity reflect a difference in the actual dream-experience of ancient and of modern man. Mr Geoffrey Gorer has pointed out to me in the interval that what we remember of our dreams largely depends on what we think worth remembering, and that in consequence ancient dream-records may present a highly simplified version of the original dream-experience.~~ On this view, what is culturally determined may be not the pattern of the dream as actually dreamt, but simply the pattern to which it conforms in memory. That, however, is by the way. I turn to describe the only long series of dreams experienced by a particular individual which has been preserved to us from the classical world.

Over the same years in which Marcus Aurelius was recording his self-examination and self-reproach his contemporary Aelius Aristides was keeping a very different sort of diary. ~~It was not a day book but what Synesius later called a 'night book': it was the night-by-night record of his dreams, which was also the record of his intercourse with the divine healer Asclepius; it included,~~ *AELIVS ARISTIDES' DREAM DIARY*

---

[1] Joel ii. 28, quoted at Acts ii. 17.

he tells us, 'cures of every kind, some conversations and continuous speeches, all sorts of visions, all Asclepius' predictions and oracles on all manner of things, some in prose, others in verse'.[1] As the years went on, these night books accumulated to the formidable total of 300,000 lines.[2] When Aristides came at last to write them up, he found them difficult to sort, as he seems to have neglected to date them; and some of them had got lost in a domestic upheaval. But out of those which remained, supplemented by his memories, he put together in no very coherent order the five extant books of his *Sacred Teachings*,[3] and was just starting on a sixth when death overtook him. They constitute the first and only religious autobiography which the pagan world has left us.

Aristides was the son of a well-to-do country gentleman in Asia Minor; he had the best education the times could offer, under the same tutor who later taught Marcus Aurelius; in his twenties he was already widely read and widely travelled, a splendid speaker and a master of the best atticising style. At the age of 26 he visited Rome and

---

[1] Aristides, *Orat.*, 48.8 Keil (all my references to the *Sacred Teachings* are to Keil's edition, now available in a reprint). The standard book on Aristides is still Boulanger's *Aelius Aristide* (1923). Cf. also Wilamowitz, 'Der Rhetor Aristeides', *Sitzb. Akad. Berl.* 1925; and on the *Sacred Teachings*, G. Misch, *Hist. of Autobiography* (Eng. trans.), II, pp. 495–510; O. Weinreich, *Neue Jahrbb.*, 33 (1914), pp. 597 ff.; Campbell Bonner, *Harv. Theol. Rev.*, 30 (1937), pp. 124–31; E. D. Phillips, *Greece and Rome*, 21 (1952), pp. 23–36; Festugière, *Personal Religion*, pp. 85–104 (including translation of many passages).

[2] *Orat.*, 48.3. Boulanger's figure of 30,000 is an oversight which others have copied from him.

[3] Ἱεροὶ Λόγοι (*Orat.*, 47–52 Keil). The conventional translation, 'Sacred Discourses', is misleading: they are not simply public addresses like most of Aristides' other writings. The title was prescribed by Asclepius in a dream (48.9), and presumably implies a divine revelation as in Hdt., 2.81.2, Plato, *Ep.* vii, 235 A, and elsewhere (cf. Festugière, *Personal Religion*, pp. 88, 168).

was presented at court; a great career in public affairs was opening before him, when he was struck down by the first of the long series of maladies which were to make him a chronic invalid for at least twelve years and transform his personality for life. Most if not all of his ailments were of the psychosomatic type: among the medley of symptoms which he reports we can recognise those of acute asthma and various forms of hypertension, producing violent nervous headaches, insomnia, and severe gastric troubles.[1] It is therefore not very surprising that the strange prescriptions which he obtained from his god in sleep should often have given at least temporary relief to the worst symptoms. His dreams themselves deserve the attention of a professional psychologist, which I hope they will one day get.

They fall into three main groups. There are the terrifying anxiety-dreams in which he is being poisoned, or chased by a bull, or attacked by barbarians; the most fully described is one where he finds himself in a long tunnel surrounded by suspicious characters with knives who are about to set on him.[2] Then there are the pathetic megalomaniac dreams, in which his spoilt career is lavishly over-compensated: bedridden by day, he converses with

---

[1] Asthma, 48.6, 48.57 (horizontal position impossible), etc.; hypertension, 49.17; headaches, 48.57; insomnia, 47.5, 48.58; digestive troubles, 47.5 and *passim*. An expert medical opinion on the case would be very welcome. It does not appear that Aristides' symptoms were ever permanently removed—perhaps because, as Festugière puts it (*Personal Religion*, p. 86), 'fundamentally, he does not want to be cured. To be cured would mean no longer to enjoy the presence and companionship of the god; and precisely what the patient needs is the companionship of the god.'

[2] *Orat.*, 47.22; cf. 47.9; 47.13; 47.54. The tunnel dream may be compared with the dream attributed to Caracalla, in which his father and brother pursue him with swords (Dio Cass., 77.15).

A MEDLEY OF
HALLUCINATIONS

emperors by night; he learns that he is to share a public memorial with Alexander the Great; secret voices assure him that he is a greater orator than Demosthenes, and (more surprisingly still) that he is Plato and Thucydides rolled into one.[1] And finally there are the countless 'divine' dreams where he meets his patron, or anyhow gets hints from him.[2] Most of these, but by no means all, are medical in content. As Aristides himself remarked, the dream-prescriptions are paradoxical, and they are often surprisingly cruel. When he is made to forswear hot baths for more than five years, compelled to run barefoot in winter, to take riverbaths in the frost and mudbaths in an icy wind, and even to make himself seasick,[3] we cannot but notice the resemblance of these divine prescriptions to the penances of Isiac devotees and the self-inflicted torments of certain Christian ascetics.[4] And we may guess that they have the same psychological origin; for these people the price of health, physical or spiritual, is the unending expiation of an unconscious guilt.

Characteristic also is the compulsion to evade some

[1] *Orat.*, 47.36–8, 46; 50.19, 49, 106; 51.59.

[2] Many very ordinary dreams are forced into the 'divine' category by ingenious interpretation: thus digging a trench is an instruction to take an emetic (47.50); a book by Menander is a warning against travelling (47.51, Μέναvδρος=μένειν τὸν ἄνδρα); reading Aristophanes' *Clouds* means rainy weather (51.18). Further examples in Festugière, *Personal Religion*, pp. 101 f. Like Artemidorus and Freud, Aristides knows that the pun is an important element in the dreamworld.

[3] *Orat.*, 47.59, 65; 48.18–23, 74–80. 'Paradoxical' nature of the prescriptions, 36.124; 42.8–9.

[4] Isiac devotees must break the ice on the wintry Tiber, Juv., 6.522. Bathing in icy water and going barefoot in all weathers are also favourite exercises of the Desert Fathers. Aristides' mudbath, though ostensibly medical in purpose, may be compared with the penitential mudbaths described by Plutarch (*De superstit.*, 7, 168 D) and those of the Egyptian ascetics in Lucian's *De morte Peregrini*, 17.

imagined threatening evil by its pre-enactment in a harmless symbolic form. Thus he must undergo a mimic shipwreck in order to escape a real one; he must sprinkle himself with dust 'in place', as he says, 'of burial, that this too might be in some fashion fulfilled'; he must even sacrifice a finger 'for the safety of the whole body', though this is eventually commuted to the sacrifice of a ring.[1] (This last example links up, if I am not mistaken, with a little boy in a dark tunnel whom bad men threaten to mutilate.)   And if these personal sacrifices are not enough to placate Destiny, he will sacrifice his friends. He tells us without a qualm how two of them on two separate occasions involuntarily played Alcestis to his Admetus and died as unconscious surrogates for his valuable life.[2]

Confronted with stuff like this, the impatient modern reader is tempted to dismiss Aristides as 'a brainsick noodle'[3] of interest only to psychiatrists. Brainsick he was, and in a not very pleasant way, yet his experience must be classed as religious; that is why I have introduced him here. He believes himself to be a man chosen by God

---

[1] *Orat.*, 48.13–14; 50.11; 48.27. The simulated burial recalls the ritual pre-enactment of death in Isiac religion (Apul., *Met.*, 11.23.7) and of burial in theurgy (Proclus, *Theol. Plat.*, 193.38 Portus). On the finger-sacrifice see Dodds, *Greeks*, ch. iv, n. 79, and George Devereux's *Reality and Dream* (1951), p. 84.

[2] *Orat.*, 48.44; 51.19–25. Such phantasies express a deep-seated feeling of guilt ('It is I who ought to have died'). Another addict of the 'divine' dream had a like experience: C. G. Jung tells us that on one occasion when gravely ill he was obsessed by the notion, founded on a dream, that the physician attending him would have to die in his stead (*Memories, Dreams, Reflections* (Eng. trans., 1963), p. 273).

[3] The phrase is Bonner's (*Harv. Theol. Rev.*, 30 (1937), p. 129); but he rightly went on to point out that Aristides had 'a religious sentiment both genuine and refined'.

as the servant and the mouthpiece (*hypokrites*) of the great Healer.[1] When Asclepius in a dream speaks to him the mystic words σὺ εἶ εἶς ('Thou art uniquely chosen'), he feels that this compensates for all his sufferings and restores meaning to his existence: henceforth he must be changed, he must be united with God and thus surpass the human condition; in this new life he adopts a new name, Theodorus, because all that is his is now the gift of God.[2] From now on he will do nothing, great or small, without the god's approval; for 'everything is nonsense compared with obedience to God'.[3] He is in fact no longer alone, imprisoned in the dreadful loneliness of the neurotic; he has found a Helper whose presence is inexpressible joy.[4]

Beginning as a medical adviser, Asclepius gradually extended his help to the whole of Aristides' life; he advises him on his reading, inspires him with brilliant ideas, presents him with the opening paragraph of a speech or the first line of a poem, and occasionally favours him with glimpses of the future, mostly in the form of short-range weather forecasts (Aristides was peculiarly sensitive to the weather).[5] How are we to interpret this curious symbiosis between man and God? A hint of the answer is perhaps contained in the dream where Aristides is confronted with his own statue and sees it change into a

[1] *Orat.*, 42.12.

[2] *Orat.*, 50.51–3. Cf. also 42.7.

[3] *Orat.*, 50.102; 51.56.

[4] Cf. the touching description of a vision of Asclepius at 48.32 (translated in Dodds, *Greeks*, p. 113).

[5] *Orat.*, 47.38; 50.24–6, 31, 39, 45. Predictions, 48.26, 48, 54, etc. For Asclepius as a patron of literature see Emma and Ludwig Edelstein, *Asclepius* (1945), II, pp. 206–8; for his mantic function, *ibid.*, pp. 104 f.

statue of Asclepius.[1] For Aristides this dream is a symbol
of his unity with his divine patron. We may perhaps see
it as symbolising the reconstruction of a broken personality which has found peace through self-identification
with the image of an ideal Father.

Aristides' relationship to Asclepius was no doubt
unique both in its intensity and in its duration. But there
was abundant precedent for it. We are assured by Celsus
that Asclepius has appeared in person to 'a great multitude
of men, both Greeks and barbarians', healing and pre-
dicting the future; and his claim is confirmed by the
numerous extant inscriptions dedicated by grateful
patients.[2] Among Aristides' contemporaries, Maximus of
Tyre had been favoured with such a vision in the waking
state; Marcus Aurelius gives thanks to the gods for 'helpful dreams' which cured him of giddiness and spitting
blood; and even the great physician Galen believes that he
has saved many lives by acting on the advice of dreams.[3]
Another contemporary was Artemidorus, who devoted
his life to collecting and classifying dreams from every
possible source, together with their interpretations.
Aristides' faith was the faith of his time—a time when, in
Eitrem's words, 'daylight reality was ceasing to be
trusted'.[4]

[1] *Orat.*, 47.17. The closest parallel I know is in Damascius, *Vit. Isidori*
(Phot., *Bibl.*, cod. 242, p. 345 a Bekker), where Damascius dreams that he is
Attis and receives cult instructions from Cybele. On 'divinisation' in general
see below, pp. 74–9.
[2] Origen, *c. Cels.*, 3.24. The inscriptions are collected and discussed in the
Edelsteins' *Asclepius*. Cf. also the important part played by dreams in Apuleius' account of the initiation of Lucius, and A. D. Nock's discussion, *Conversion*, ch. ix.
[3] Max. Tyr., 9.7; M. Ant., 1.17.9; Galen, vol. XVI, p. 222 Kühn.
[4] S. Eitrem, *Orakel und Mysterien am Ausgang der Antike* (1947), p. 52.

The Christian attitude to dreams was not in principle different, save that for medical purposes incubation at a shrine of Asclepius was replaced by incubation at the shrine of a martyr or saint—a practice which obtains in Greece to this day.[1] Dreams of religious content were, as we should expect, frequent in the early Church, and were taken very seriously. When a Bishop dreams that the Last Judgement is at hand, the faithful cease to cultivate their fields and devote themselves entirely to prayer. According to Origen, many have been converted to Christianity by dreams or waking visions.[2] For others a dream marked a crisis in their spiritual life: Natalius the Confessor was saved from heresy by a dream in which holy angels whipped him all night long; Gregory of Nyssa was turned to a life of contemplation by a dream in which the Forty Martyrs scolded him for his remissness; a dream convinced Augustine's friend, the physician Gennadius, of the immortality of the soul; and even so practical a man as Cyprian seems to have acted constantly at the monition of dreams.[3] The most influential of all recorded dreams is, I suppose, the one in which Constantine beheld the magical monogram *chi rho*, and was told 'hoc signo

---

[1] Cf. E. Lucius, *Die Anfänge des Heiligenkults* (1904), pp. 252–70; L. Deubner, *De incubatione* (1900), pp. 56 ff.; B. Schmidt, *Das Volksleben der Neugriechen* (1871), pp. 77–82; J. C. Lawson, *Modern Greek Folklore and Ancient Greek Religion* (1910), p. 302. The Montanists practised incubation at Pepuza, the predestined site of the New Jerusalem (Epiphanius, *Haer.*, 49.1–2).

[2] Hippolytus, *In Dan.*, 4.19; Origen, *c. Cels.*, 1.46. For action in obedience to a dream Christians had the example of St Paul, Acts xvi. 9 f.

[3] Eus., *Hist. Eccl.*, 5.28.8–12; Greg. Nyss., *In xl martyres* (*P.G.* 46, 784 D–785 B; Augustine, *Epist. ad Evodium*, 159.3; Cyprian, *Epist.* 11.3–4 (cf. Harnack, *Z.N.T.W.*, 3 (1902), pp. 177–91). Further examples are quoted by Labriolle, *Crise*, p. 342.

victor eris', on the eve of the battle of the Milvian Bridge.[1]
I cannot here enter into the discussion which has raged
over this dream; but we need not adopt the rationalistic
view of nineteenth-century historians, who saw in it a
statesmanlike invention designed to impress the mob.[2]
There is independent evidence that Constantine shared
the superstitions of his subjects;[3] but like Cyprian he was
perfectly capable of combining a superstitious faith with
a practical awareness of administrative needs. His dream
did indeed serve a useful purpose, but that does not prove
it a fiction: dreams *are* purposive, as we now know.

But from a psychological point of view the most interesting Christian dreams recorded in our period are those
attributed to St Perpetua, a 22-year-old married woman
who was martyred at Carthage in the year 202-3. I say
'attributed' because martyrologies are a highly suspect
class of literature, and the *Passio Perpetuae*[4] needs discus-

[1] This is the almost contemporary account given by Lactantius, *De mort.
pers.*, 44. Many years later Constantine in his old age recalled an appearance
seen in the sky one afternoon in Gaul 'by himself and the whole army', linked
it with his dream, and told Eusebius about it (Eus., *Vit. Const.*, 1.28). Here
one must suspect secondary elaboration of a *bona fide* memory. No doubt
something unusual *was* seen that afternoon: celestial phenomena (halos, par-
helia, etc.) were anxiously observed at times of crisis, and are often recorded as
portents by Livy. But this portent can scarcely have been interpreted in a
Christian sense *at the time of its occurrence*; otherwise Lactantius could hardly
fail to know of it and his silence would be very strange.—The *chi rho* was a
χαρακτήρ which could frighten demons, Lact., *Div. inst.*, 4.27.1.
[2] Against the rationalising view see N. H. Baynes, 'Constantine the Great
and the Christian Church', *Proc. Brit. Acad.*, 15 (1929-31); A. Alföldi, *The Conversion of Constantine and Pagan Rome* (Eng. trans., 1948), ch. ii; A. H. M. Jones
in Momigliano, *Conflict*, pp. 33 f.
[3] The foundation of Constantinople was commanded by a dream (*Cod.
Theod.*, 13.5.7; Sozomen, *Hist. Eccl.*, 2.3.3).
[4] Latest edition by C. van Beek (1936), with introduction and commentary.
Modern critical discussion starts from the first publication of the Greek text by
Harris and Gifford in 1890. Among the more important contributions are
those of J. A. Robinson, *Texts and Studies*, I, ii (1891); L. Duchesne, *C. R.*

sion before we accept its evidence. It is built round two first-person documents. One of these purports to be a sort of prison diary kept by Perpetua while awaiting execution; it includes a detailed account of four dreams, with their attendant circumstances. The other consists of a vision recounted in the person of Satyrus, who was martyred on the same occasion. To these documents an anonymous redactor has added a list of the martyrs, a few facts about Perpetua, and a long account of the actual martyrdom. The whole thing has come down to us both in a Latin and in a Greek version. The majority of the Church historians who have discussed the *Passio* have accepted without question the veracity of the redactor and the authenticity of the incapsulated documents; but so good a judge as Eduard Schwartz thought that both documents were forged by the redactor.[1] To me the different elements of the piece seem to be of very unequal value. The redactor's gory and edifying narrative does not inspire me with confidence, particularly as it is in direct conflict with the bald and sober factual account given in the later *Acta Perpetuae*.[2] The redactor tells us that he composed it

Acad. Inscr., iv, 19 (1891–2), pp. 39 ff.; Harnack, *Gesch. d. altchr. Lit.*, II, ii, 1904, pp. 321–4; Pio Franchi de' Cavalieri, *Röm. Quartalschrift*, 5 (1896), Suppl.-Band; Labriolle, *Crise*, pp. 338 ff.; and E. Rupprecht, *Rh. Mus.*, 90 (1941), pp. 177–92.

[1] E. Schwartz, 'De Pionio et Polycarpo' (Progr. Göttingen, 1905), p. 23. The same view was taken by Stählin, *Geschichte d. griech. Lit.*, II, ii, 1913, p. 1079. First-person narrative was a familiar fictional form, much used not only in Greek novels but in Christian apocrypha (cf. R. Söder, *Die apokryphen Apostel-geschichten u. d. romanhafte Literatur der Antike*, 1932, pp. 211 f.).

[2] The *Acta* as a whole admittedly merits even less confidence than the *Passio* as a whole, since it gets the date of the martyrdom wrong by over half a century. But its author, who evidently had the *Passio* before him, must have had some good reason to reject its picturesque account of the happenings in the arena and substitute a plain and unexciting statement—incompatible with the *Passio*—about which martyr was thrown to which kind of beast.

by permission of the Holy Spirit, and it would seem that the Spirit must have supplied him with many of his details—incidents and conversations which could scarcely have come to the notice of the spectators. Moreover, as in the Gospel narratives, certain incidents appear to have been introduced in order to provide a fulfilment of prophecy.[1] However, the historicity of his account does not directly concern us. I am equally doubtful about the vision of Satyrus.[2] But there are several good reasons for believing that Perpetua's prison diary is substantially a genuine document.

In the first place, Perpetua's simple style is very different from the rhetorical cleverness of the redactor, which has led some scholars to identify him with Tertullian.[3] And while I

[1] In Perpetua's dream Satyrus preceded her up the ladder, so Satyrus must die before she does. In her dream of the arena her adversary carried a sword, so after she has been mauled by a 'mad cow' a sword must be used to despatch her, though according to the *Acta* she was eaten by a lion. One purpose of the *Passio*, perhaps its main purpose, is to prove that the Holy Spirit is still active in the Church.

[2] This vision has no setting whatever; we are not told when or in what circumstances Satyrus experienced it. And it is full of conventional Christian imagery—angels carrying off the soul, other still greater angels of the Presence, walls of light, voices crying 'Holy, holy, holy!', elders arranged in a neat row on either side of the Throne. This is what we expect to find in a literary apocalypse of mediocre originality. The vision may in fact have been designed as a counterweight to Perpetua's unorthodoxy (we notice that instead of eating cheese the spirits in Satyrus' Heaven feed on the odour of sanctity). But another motive is also apparent: in the curious scene with Bishop Optatus and the Elder Aspasius (c. 13) the author deals these contemporary dignitaries a resounding smack in the face—until they settle their quarrels, and until Optatus manages his flock better, they will be shut out from Heaven. Revelation here merges into polemic; the vision of the next world becomes a literary device for satirising unpopular figures in this one, as it occasionally is in Hermas' *Shepherd*. If the author of the *Passio* had decided, like the author of the *Acta*, to omit the vision of Satyrus, we should not, I think, have missed much of psychological or religious value.

[3] Stylistic similarities between the redactor and Tertullian were listed by Labriolle. But I feel, with Rupprecht, that serious doubt is cast on the

take it as now pretty well established that the redactor's original language was Latin, there are fairly strong reasons for thinking that the diary was originally kept in Greek.[1]

Secondly, the diary is entirely free from marvels, and the dreams it reports are entirely dreamlike. Unlike the vision of Satyrus, they are given in their day-to-day setting, as part of the experience of prison life. The first three are 'sought' dreams; they were induced by prayer.[2] The first and last picture her coming martyrdom, the first under the image of escaping from a snake up a dangerous

identification by the inaccuracy of Tertullian's solitary mention of the *Passio*, his reference to Perpetua's dream at *De anima*, 55.4, which would seem to be in fact a reference to the vision of Satyrus (11.9; 13.8)—for even if he wrote 'martyras' and not 'commartyras' his language is hardly justified by Perpetua's mention of 'candidati' at *Passio*, 4.8. Ancient authors frequently misquote the writings of others, but they are less likely to misquote their own. It may be added that the authorship of the *Passio* was unknown to Augustine (*De nat. animae*, 1, 10 (12)).

[1] After I had reached this conclusion I found that it had been anticipated by Harnack (*loc. cit.*) and by W. Kroll, *Glotta*, 13 (1924), 283. There are a number of good reasons for thinking that the redactor wrote originally in Latin— notably the play on *salvus* in c. 21, which is lost in the Greek. And the statement of 'Satyrus' that Perpetua spoke Greek in Heaven (13.4) suggests a Latin original here also. In Perpetua's diary, on the other hand, the Latin is in several places less appropriate than the Greek, and looks as if it originated through misreading of (or corruption in) a Greek manuscript: at 4.7, *quasi* for ὡς εἰς (misread as ὡς εἰ); at 6.1, *cum pranderemus* for ἐν ῇ ὥριστο (mistaken for some part of ἀριστάω); and especially at 8.2, the entirely unsuitable *trahebat* for ἔρρεεν (misread as εἴρυεν). That Perpetua should write her diary in Greek is not surprising, since 'Satyrus' knows her as a Greek speaker and her brother has a Greek name. The family was doubtless bilingual, like many in Roman Africa.

[2] Persons awaiting martyrdom were thought to be in especially close touch with the Supernatural (cf. Acts vii. 55 f.), and if they shared this belief they would naturally expect god-sent dreams. Examples of dreams and visions said to have been experienced by martyrs in prison are quoted by E. le Blant, *Les Persécutions et les martyres aux premiers siècles de notre ère* (1893), pp. 88 ff.—For most of the arguments in this paragraph and the next I am indebted to Marie-Louise von Franz, 'Die Passio Perpetuae', printed as an appendix to C. G. Jung's book *Aion*, 1951 (in the German edition only). I cannot, however, follow her in her Jungian interpretation of the individual dreams.

ladder to a place where she meets a heavenly shepherd, the last under that of a fight with the Devil in the person of a hideous Egyptian whom she triumphantly defeats. The second and third are concerned with her long-dead baby brother Deinocrates, who had already, to her surprise, forced himself into her waking consciousness on the day preceding his appearance in her dreams. He presumably represents an element in the Unconscious which is demanding attention. This is the sort of detail which a forger would hardly invent. And the dreams themselves have the true dreamlike inconsequence. The shepherd in the first dream milks *cheese*, or rather curds, direct from his sheep and gives it her to eat—the sort of time-compression which is common in dreams. And in the fourth dream Perpetua suddenly finds herself transformed into a man; this again is scarcely the sort of detail which would occur to a hagiographer.[1]

Furthermore, these dreams have little of the specifically Christian colouring which we should expect to find in a pious fiction (and which we do find in the vision of Satyrus). Cheese-eating in Heaven is quite unorthodox, and I doubt if it has anything to do with the obscure heretical sect known as 'bread-and-cheesers' (Artotyrites); they are first mentioned nearly two centuries later, and in a quite different part of the world;[2] moreover the essen-

---

[1] In the Gnostic *Gospel of Thomas* we read that women can enter the Kingdom of Heaven only by becoming men (112: cf. Clem., *Exc. ex Theod.*, 21.3; Hipp., *Haer.*, 5.8.44). But we need not credit Perpetua with this heretical opinion: change of sex in dreams is not rare, and Perpetua has to be a man in order to engage in a gladiatorial combat.

[2] See Labriolle, *Crise*, pp. 343 f. As Devereux points out to me, the 'curds' offered by a male personage at the top of a 'ladder' could well have a latent sexual meaning. Cf. the conscious use of this symbolism at Job x. 10, with Jastrow's note.

tial element of bread is missing in the dream. The ladder has parallels in Aristides' dreams,[1] as well as in Mithraism; and the dream of Deinocrates' sufferings is based less on Christian pictures of Purgatory than on ancient pagan notions about the thirsty dead and the fate of those who die untimely.[2] In the final dream the Supreme Judge is pictured not as Christ but as an umpire or trainer of gladiators; and the reward of the victor is not the martyr's crown but the golden apples of the Hesperides. This pagan imagery is entirely natural in the dreams of a quite recent convert; it would be surprising in a propagandist apocalypse.

I conclude, then, that in the prison diary we have an authentic first-hand narrative of the last days of a gallant martyr. It is a touching record of humanity and courage, quite free from the pathological self-importance of an Ignatius or an Aristides. Perpetua has been instructively compared[3] with another Christian martyr, Sophie Scholl, who at about the same age was put to death by the Nazis. Miss Scholl also had a dream as she lay in prison on the last night of her life: she thought that she was climbing a steep mountain, carrying in her arms a child to be baptised; eventually she fell into a crevasse, but the child was saved.

---

[1] Cf. especially *Orat.*, 49.48, an alarming dream about ladders 'stretching below and above the earth and marking the power of the god in each domain'; Aristides calls it a τελετή. He has another frightening dream about ladders at 51.65, and at 48.30 Philadelphus dreams of 'a sacred ladder and a divine presence' (but at 47.48 the ladder obviously symbolises worldly advancement). Jacob's ladder appears less relevant; and the Byzantine ladder-pictures showing the ascent of the souls belong to a later age (they were inspired by the *Ladder* of St John Climacus).

[2] Cf. F. J. Dölger, 'Antike Parallelen zum leidenden Deinokrates', *Ant. u. Christ.*, II (1930).

[3] By Frl. von Franz, in C. G. Jung, *Aion*.

The mountain with its crevasses corresponds to Perpetua's dangerous ladder; the unbaptised infant recalls Deinocrates, who died unbaptised[1] at the age of seven. For both dreamers the child is saved, and their maternal hearts are comforted. But whereas Perpetua dreams of a Good Shepherd and a symbolic victory in the arena, Sophie Scholl is content to see herself fall into the abyss: faith in a miraculous future is a harder thing in the twentieth century than it was in the third.

I must now turn to consider a different type of 'daemonic' personality—the man or woman to or through whom a supernatural being speaks in the daytime. In our society such persons function most often, though not always, as 'spirit mediums'. The Polynesians call them 'god-boxes'. In antiquity they went under a variety of names. If you believed in their pronouncements, you called them *prophetai*, 'spokesmen for the supernatural',[2] or *entheoi*, 'filled with god'; if you didn't, they were 'demon-ridden' (*daimonontes*), which put them in the same class as epileptics and paranoiacs. Or you could use the neutral psychological term *ekstatikoi*, which could be applied to any one in whom the normal state of consciousness was temporarily or permanently disturbed. The vulgar word was *engastrimuthoi*, 'belly-talkers'. The

[1] Augustine argued on theological grounds that Deinocrates must have been baptised, else he could not have been saved (*De nat. animae*, 1, 10 (12)). But the 'piscina' in the dreams surely stands for the baptismal font; moreover the child's father was a pagan, and Perpetua herself had only recently been baptised.

[2] This is the original sense of the word, and remained the standard one: its history has been examined by E. Fascher, Προφήτης (1927). The gift of foreknowledge was a frequent but not a necessary attribute of the *prophetes*. προφητεύειν in the sense 'to predict' and προφητεία in the sense of 'prediction' are almost confined to Jewish and Christian writers (Fascher, p. 148).

New Testament and the early Fathers use *prophetai* and sometimes *pneumatikoi*, 'filled with the Spirit', though the latter term had also a wider application.[1] All these words are or can be descriptive of the same psychological type— the person who is subject to attacks of dissociation. Ancient observers recognised, as we do, two degrees of dissociation, one in which the subject's normal consciousness persists side by side with the intrusive personality, and on the other hand a deeper trance in which the normal self is completely suppressed, so that it retains no memory of what was said or done.[2] In the former case the subject may simply report what the intrusive voice is saying; in the latter the voice speaks in the first person through the subject's lips, as 'Apollo' professes to do at Delphi or Claros. In antiquity the intruder normally claimed to be a god or daemon; only in exceptional cases did it profess to be a deceased human being,[3] as in modern spiritualism: contact with the supernatural was more desired than contact with dead friends or relatives.

[1] On the meaning of ἐκστατικός see below, pp. 70–2.; on ἐγγαστρίμυθοι, Dodds, *Greeks*, pp. 71 f. and notes. Iamblichus, *De myst.*, 3.7, rejects the term ἔκστασις as describing at best a secondary effect; what is primary is possession (κατέχεσθαι). From 3.19 *init.* it is clear that he would also reject the modern term 'medium'. The many senses in which the words πνεῦμα and πνευματικός were used by philosophical, medical, Jewish and Christian writers have been elaborately studied by G. Verbeke, *L'Évolution de la doctrine du Pneuma du Stoïcisme à S. Augustin* (1945); see also the instructive discussion by Edwyn Bevan, *Symbolism and Belief* (1938), Lectures vii and viii.

[2] Iamb., *De myst.*, 3.5; Cassian, *Collationes*, 7.12; Psellus, *Scripta minora*, I, 248.1 ff. (based on Proclus). Cf. Dodds, *Greeks*, pp. 297, 309 n. 116.

[3] Usually the earthbound soul of a βιαιοθάνατος (Tert., *De anima*, 5.7; Eunap., *Vit. soph.*, 473 Boissonade). Justin, *Apol. i*, 18, speaks of persons who are possessed by the souls of the dead, but adds that they are usually said to be possessed by demons and crazy. Porphyry, *apud* Iamb., *De myst.*, 2.3, asks with reference to apparitions how we can distinguish the presence of a god, an angel, an archangel, a daemon, an *archon* (planetary spirit), or a human soul.

The reasons for this desire were not necessarily religious; they were often purely practical Then as now, these secondary personalities were credited with occult powers: they could heal the sick; they could speak the language of angels;[1] they could read the thoughts of the inquirer or the contents of a sealed letter; they became aware of distant events; above all, they could foretell the future.[2] The prestige of the official oracles had long been declining;[3] and although imperial patronage produced a

[1] Alexander of Abonutichus utters 'unintelligible vocables which sounded like Hebrew or Phoenician' (Lucian, *Alex.*, 13); and the meaningless formulae which occur in magical papyri have sometimes been taken for transcripts of glossolalia. Otherwise this seems to have been a Christian speciality, from the days of St Paul (who thought the Corinthian Church overdid it, 1 Cor. xiv) down to those of Irenaeus, late in the second century, who tells us that 'many brethren in the Church have prophetic gifts and through the Spirit speak in all manner of tongues' (*Haer.*, 5.6.1). The Corinthian 'tongues' are understood only by God (1 Cor. xiv. 2): they are accordingly no human speech; they are like the Martian language invented by Helène Smith and described by T. Flournoy, *Des Indes à la planète Mars* (1900). The author of Acts, ii, on the other hand, interpreted the phenomenon as one of 'xenoglossy', speaking in human languages unknown to the speaker. For this too there are plenty of alleged parallels, from Herodotus (8.135) down to the feats attributed to certain modern 'mediums'. On the whole subject see the excellent book of E. Lombard, *De la glossolalie chez les premiers chrétiens* (1910).

[2] Thought-reading, 1 Cor. xiv. 24; Tac., *Ann.*, 2.54 (Claros); Plut., *De garr.*, 20 (Delphi); Aug., *c. Acad.*, 1.6 f. Reading sealed letter, Lucian, *Alex.*, 21; Macrob., *Sat.*, 1.23.14 f.; *P.G.M.*, iii, 371, v, 301. Awareness of distant events, Dio Cass., 67.18 (Philostr., *Vit. Apoll.*, 8.26 ff.); Eunap., *Vit. soph.*, 470 Boiss.; Aug., *De Gen. ad litt.*, 12.27. Precognition, Acts xi. 27 f., xxi. 10 f.; Philostr., *Vit. Apoll.*, 4.18; Origen, *c. Cels.*, 1.46; etc. Cf. my paper in *Greek Poetry and Life, essays presented to Gilbert Murray* (1936), pp. 364 ff. (repr. in *J. of Parapsychology*, 10 (1946), pp. 290 ff.).

[3] Cic., *De Div.*, 1.38; 2.117; Strabo, 9.3.8; Plut., *Def. orac.*, 5. At the end of the second century Clement of Alexandria claims that the *official* oracles are dead, though he admits that private 'mediums' (ἐγγαστρίμυθοι) are still popular with the masses (*Protrept.*, 2.11.1 f.). An oracle quoted by Porphyry, *Phil. ex orac.*, p. 172 Wolff (=Eus., *Praep. Evang.*, 5.15), asserts that the only surviving oracular shrines are those of Apollo at Didyma, Delphi and Claros: is this designed as a warning to unauthorised competitors? On astrology as the successor of Delphi see Juvenal, 6.553 ff.

revival in the second century, they never (with the possible exception of Claros) fully recovered their old popularity. The reason was not that human curiosity or human credulity had diminished, but that competition had increased. Astrology was one important rival; and there were also many written revelations of the future, like the *Sibylline Oracles* and the numerous Christian and Gnostic apocalypses. Augustus is said to have caused over two thousand copies of prophetic books, anonymous or pseudonymous, to be collected and burnt.[1] Moreover, the old religious centres no longer had a monopoly of *prophetai*. Alexander of Abonutichus[2] showed how easy it was to start a new oracle from scratch with an entirely new god and to build up a flourishing business with the help of a few good connections (his daughter married the Governor of Asia); the only serious opposition came from the Epicureans and the Christians. And from the third century onwards there is evidence of a greatly increased use of private mediums—those whom Minucius Felix calls 'prophets without a temple'.[3] The magical papyri offer recipes for throwing such persons into the requisite state of trance.[4] Many of the 'oracles' quoted by Porphyry appear to come from sources of this kind; and private mediumship was systematically exploited by the

---

[1] Suet., *Div. August.*, 31.

[2] Cf. O. Weinreich, *N. Jahrbb.*, 47 (1921), pp. 129 ff.; A. D. Nock, *C.Q.*, 22 (1928), pp. 160 ff., and *Conversion*, pp. 93 ff.; S. Eitrem, *Orakel und Mysterien*, ch. viii; M. Caster, *Études sur Alexandre* (thèse suppl., 1938). The last-named includes text and translation of Lucian's *Alexandros*, with commentary.

[3] *Oct.*, 27, *Vates absque templo*; they correspond to Clement's ἐγγαστρί-μυθοι (see above, p. 55, n. 3).

[4] *P.G.M.*, i, 850–929; vii, 540 ff.; viii, 1 ff. Apuleius, *Apol.*, 42, Justin, *Apol. i*, 18, and Origen, *De princ.*, 3.3.3, refer to the use of boy 'mediums' for this purpose.

theurgists whose scripture was the theosophical farrago
known as the *Chaldaean Oracles.*

No doubt much of the increasing demand for oracles
simply reflects the increasing insecurity of the times. This
is illustrated by a papyrus containing a list of 21 inquiries
addressed to some oracle late in the third century: they
include such questions as, 'Am I to become a beggar?',
'Shall I be sold up?', 'Should I take to flight?', 'Shall I get
my salary?', 'Am I under a spell?'[1] But this is not the
only type of question which interested people in our
period. Sometime in the second or the third century one
Theophilus put a less personal problem to the oracle of
Claros:[2] 'Are you God,' he asked, 'or is some one else
God?' It sounds a little naive to us: 'Question de Dieu,
cela manque d'actualité', as the French editor wrote on
the rejection slip. But to the men of that age the question
was real and important—and where else should one turn
for an answer save to an inspired *prophetes*? Claros duly
provided an answer: the supreme God, it said, was Aion,
'Eternity': Apollo was only one of his 'angels' or mes-
sengers. 'Doctrinal' oracles of this novel sort were a
feature of the time.[3] Apart from these, *prophetai* exercised
a serious religious influence mainly in two contexts—

[1] *P. Oxy.* 1477: cf. Rostovtzeff, *Soc. and Econ. Hist. of the Roman Empire*
427. In *P. Oxy.* 925 a Christian addresses an equally personal question to
Christ. For other examples from the papyri, pagan and Christian, see B. R.
Rees, 'Popular Religion in Graeco-Roman Egypt, II', *J. Eg. Arch.*, 36 (1950),
p. 87.

[2] *Theosophia Tubingensis*, no. 13 Buresch (also reproduced in Wolff's edition
of Porph., *Phil. ex orac.*, pp. 231 ff., and in H. Lewy's *Chaldaean Oracles and
Theurgy*, pp. 18 f.). I cannot agree with Lewy's view that the ascription to
Claros is necessarily erroneous, or with his translation of the oracle: see *Harv.
Theol. Rev.*, 54 (1961), p. 266.

[3] See A. D. Nock, *R.E.A.*, 30 (1928), pp. 280 ff.; Eitrem, *Orakel und Mysterien*, ch. vi. Cf. Porphyry's oracles about Christ (below, pp. 107 f.).

Christianity (including Christian Gnosticism) and theurgy.

I have written about theurgy elsewhere, and as its fullest development falls outside our period I shall not discuss it here. In the earliest Church the claim of the *prophetai* to speak by inspiration of the Holy Spirit was generally accepted, being firmly based on Scripture: the *pneuma* had descended on the Apostles, and would continue until the Last Day; Christ himself was said to have predicted its coming.[1] As in pagan prophecy, the *pneuma* might speak in the first person through its human instrument: we have an example at Acts xiii. 2. Naturally some form of control was needed to ensure that the inspiration really came from the *pneuma* and not from a demon. The discerning of spirits was thought by St Paul to be a special gift. In practice, the control seems to have been at first chiefly moral: so long as the itinerant *prophetes* lives humbly and asks nothing for himself, he is probably all right; but the *Didache* warns against false prophets who are inspired to demand money or a good dinner, and Hermas against those who court popularity by telling fortunes.[2] Celsus

[1] Acts ii; Ephes. iv. 11 ff.; John xvi. 12 f.; Eus., *Hist. Eccl.*, 5.17.4. Cf. W. Schepelern, *Der Montanismus und die phrygischen Kulte* (Germ. trans., 1929), pp. 152 ff.; F. Pfister in *R.A.C.*, s.v. 'Ekstase', pp. 981 f.

[2] I Cor. xii. 10; *Didache*, 11; Hermas, *Pastor*, Mand. 11. In the Christian view, 'prophecy' ought not to be a profession (cf. e.g. Aristides, *Apol.*, 11.1); its proper place was at a religious meeting. For condemnation of false prophets on doctrinal grounds, cf. 1 Tim. iv. 1 ff., where the author, campaigning against Gnosticism, warns his readers against 'evil spirits who forbid marriage'. The Gnostic teachers appear to have relied heavily on *prophetai*: thus Basileides appealed to the authority of the prophets Barcabbas and Barcoph 'and others whom he called by barbarous names' (Eus., *Hist. Eccl.*, 4.7.7); his son Isidore expounded the prophet Parchor (perhaps identical with Barcoph?), according to Clement, *Strom.*, 6.6.53; Apelles based his *Phaneroseis* on the revelations of a prophetess named Philoumene (Tert., *De praescr.*, 6.6, 30.6; *De carne Christi*, 6.1; Eus., *Hist. Eccl.*, 5.13.2), though in old age he seems to have reached the conclusion that all prophets were unreliable (Eus., *ibid.*, 5.13.5 f.).

knows of false *prophetai* 'in the region of Phoenicia and Palestine' who 'prophesy at the slightest excuse for some trivial cause both inside and outside temples'; according to Celsus they actually claim to be God or the Son of God or the Holy Spirit, but no doubt that claim was made by the voice speaking through them in the first person. Celsus has talked to some of them and they have confessed to being impostors.[1] They have sometimes been taken for Montanists, but on the usual dating of Celsus and of Montanus it looks a little too early for Montanists to be found in that part of the world.[2]

It is a great pity that no *prophetes*, pagan or Christian, has left us a record of his experience comparable to the *Sacred Teachings* of Aristides. Neither a fictitious romance like Philostratus' *Life of Apollonius* nor an artificial allegory like Hermas's *Shepherd* tells us much about real *prophetai*. The only possible specimens of the class of whom we have contemporary biographies are Alexander and Peregrinus;[3] and since both biographies are bitterly hostile it is hard to tell how much is history and how much malicious invention. If we are to believe Lucian, Alexander's story is a simple case of successful fraud on the public. Peregrinus is a much more complex and more interesting

[1] Origen, *c. Cels.*, 7.8–9, 11.

[2] Cf. Labriolle, *Crise*, pp. 95 ff. Neither Celsus nor Montanus, however, can be dated with certainty. These persons have also been taken for pagan *prophetai*; but Celsus would hardly blunder to that extent, and the formula θεὸs ἢ θεοῦ παῖs ἢ πνεῦμα θεῖον surely points to Christianity.

[3] On Lucian's *Alexandros* see above, p. 56, n. 2. His *De morte Peregrini* has been edited with a commentary by J. Schwartz (1951). Peregrinus has been discussed by Zeller, *Vorträge*, II (1877), pp. 154 ff.; Bernays, *Lucian und die Kyniker* (1879); D. R. Dudley, *History of Cynicism* (1937), pp. 170 ff.; M. Caster, *Lucien et la pensée religieuse* (1937), pp. 237 ff.; K. von Fritz, *P.-W.*, s.v.; and others.

character, and his career as narrated by Lucian is a very strange one.

Born of wealthy parents at Parium on the Hellespont, he gets into trouble as a young man through disreputable love affairs, quarrels with his father, and leaves home under suspicion of having strangled him. In Palestine he is converted to Christianity and becomes a *prophetes* and a leader in the community; he expounds the Scriptures and writes numerous books himself. Gaoled as a Christian, he wins great credit by his stubborn refusal to renounce his faith, but is eventually released by an enlightened Governor. Next, he goes home, voluntarily, to face charges of parricide, but silences his accusers by presenting the whole of his estates to the town for charitable purposes.[1] For a time he is supported by the Christians, but he quarrels with them[2] and is reduced to asking, unsuccessfully, for the return of his estates. After this he visits Egypt, where he practises flagellation, smears his face with mud, and adopts the Cynic way of life in its crudest form.[3] From there he goes to Italy, whence he is

[1] As von Fritz suggests, Lucian has probably confused the order of events here. If Peregrinus had been still a Christian at this time, he would scarcely have returned home in Cynic garb as Lucian describes (*Peregr.*, 15), and he would have given his estates to the Church rather than to a heathen municipality. For surrender of wealth by pagans cf. Philostr., *Vit. Apoll.*, 1.13; Porph., *Vit. Plot.*, 7.

[2] *Peregr.*, 16. The occasion of the breach is unknown. Lucian's suggestion that Peregrinus had broken a Christian food-taboo is put forward only as a guess, and does not seem very probable. So stout a 'confessor' would scarcely eat meat sacrificed to pagan deities (as Labriolle assumes, *Réaction*, p. 104), still less the Hecate-sacrifices at the crossroads (Schwartz), which were officially taboo to everybody and are therefore excluded by Lucian's words. Nock's statement that he was found to be guilty of immoral conduct (*Conversion*, p. 220) is not supported by the text of Lucian.

[3] Christian and Cynic asceticism had a good deal in common: voluntary poverty was characteristic of both, and Aristides thought them both peculiar

expelled for insulting the Emperor; once again his indifference to personal danger wins him admirers. We next find him settled in Greece, where he attempts to start a rising against the Roman power and publicly insults the philanthropic benefactor Herodes Atticus, Finally he crowns his career by a sensational suicide, burning himself to death before an admiring crowd at the Olympic Festival of A.D. 165. Whereupon he becomes the object of a cult: the stick he once carried sells for a talent;[1] a statue set up in his honour works miracles (as a Christian writer testifies[2]) and attracts pilgrims in great numbers.

What are we to make of this extraordinary life-history, of which the main facts are probably correct, though we need not accept the interpretations Lucian puts on them? Lucian would explain everything in it, from first to last, by a morbid craving for notoriety; and we should probably accept from him that Peregrinus was, among other things, an exhibitionist.[3] We might be tempted, in fact, to conclude that he was more than a little mad. Yet Aulus

in combining the opposite vices of αὐθάδεια and ταπεινότης, along with contempt for traditional religion (*Orat.*, 46 Dind., p. 402). Cf. Bernays, pp. 30–9; Reitzenstein, *Hell. Wund.*, pp. 64–74. Hippolytus, *Haer.*, 10.18, describes Tatian's way of life as a κυνικώτερος βίος, and the story of the Christian ascetic Sarapion (*Hist. Laus.*, 37, p. 109 Butler) abounds in the grossest Cynic traits.

[1] Lucian, *Adv. indoct.*, 14.

[2] Athenagoras, *Legat.*, 26; cf. *Peregr.*, 41, evidently a *praedictio post eventum*. It may have been the emergence of this new cult which moved Lucian to write his angry pamphlet, possibly in reply to one published by Peregrinus' disciple Theagenes (cf. Reitzenstein, *Hell. Wund.*, p. 50, and Caster, *Lucien*, p. 242).

[3] Craving for notoriety, *Peregr.*, 1; 14; 20. Literal exhibitionism, *Peregr.*, 17. The latter is a traditional Cynic trait (Diog. Laert., 6.46, etc.), and it may be only Lucian's malice which ascribes it to Peregrinus; but it fits the man's general character well enough to be credible.

Gellius, who knew him in his Greek period, found him 'a serious and steadfast person', who 'had many profitable and improving things to say';[1] and even Lucian testifies that he was thought of as 'a second Socrates' or 'a second Epictetus'[2]—apparently on moral rather than philosophical grounds. This may encourage us to look a little deeper into his personality than Lucian chose to do. A possible clue may be found in the appalling charge of parricide which hung over him all his life. He runs away from it; he returns to face it; and it is surely recalled in his unexpected last words, 'Spirits of my mother and my father, receive me with kindness'.[3] We need not believe the charge to be literally true; but that certain memories weighed heavy on him is suggested not only by those last words but by the sermon which Aulus Gellius heard him preach at Athens, whose burden was, 'Your secret sins shall find you out'.[4] If this is so, it may help us to understand better than Lucian did the two conspicuous features of his career—his hostile attitude to authority and his determination to be a martyr. For what it is worth, I am

[1] Aulus Gellius, *Noctes Atticae*, 12.11.

[2] *Peregr.*, 12; 18. Ammianus, 29.1.39, calls him 'philosophus clarus'.

[3] *Peregr.*, 36. Lucian suggests no very convincing motive for the suicide. Peregrinus' followers thought that he was emulating 'the Brahmans' (25; 38); they may have had in mind the inscription at Athens recording the suicide of an Indian who leapt on to the pyre ἑαυτὸν ἀπαθανατίσας (Nic. Dam., *apud* Strabo, 15.1.73; Plut., *Alex.*, 69). One might be tempted to compare the recent public 'fire-suicides' of Buddhist monks in Saigon. These, however, were designed as acts of protest against religious discrimination; if Peregrinus had any comparable motive, Lucian has suppressed it.

[4] Gellius, *Noctes Atticae*, 12.11. When Peregrinus quoted the Sophoclean lines,

πρὸς ταῦτα κρύπτε μηδέν, ὡς ὁ πάνθ᾽ ὁρῶν
καὶ πάντ᾽ ἀκούων πάντ᾽ ἀναπτύσσει χρόνος

(fr. 280 Nauck = 301 Pearson), may he not have had his own case in mind?

disposed to guess that both these traits had their origin in his unhappy early relations with his father: he must resist the paternalism of the Governor of Syria, of Antoninus Pius, of Herodes Atticus; like a good leveller, he must flout every convention; but he must also punish himself by poverty, by flagellation, in the end by death, for the violence he has done to the dominating father-image.

If I am right, we must see Peregrinus as an individual rather than a type. In any case, in his capacity as a Christian *prophetes* we can scarcely be said to see him at all: Lucian knew little about Christian practices, and cared less. If we wish to form some notion of Christian 'prophetic' utterances, we had better turn to those ascribed to Montanus, despite the fact that like Peregrinus he was eventually rejected by the Church, and that in his case too we are dependent for precise information largely on hostile sources.[1] A Phrygian by birth, Montanus is said to have been a priest either of Apollo or of Magna Mater before his conversion to Christianity; but it does not appear that his prophecy owed much to his Phrygian origins.[2] It was probably about the year 172[3] that a voice, not his own, began to speak in the first person through

[1] The sources are collected in P. de Labriolle's *Les Sources de l'histoire du Montanisme* (1913) and discussed in his *Crise*; for the utterances of the Voice see *Crise*, ch. ii.

[2] This is the negative conclusion of Schepelern's *Der Montanismus und die phrygischen Kulte*. Montanism grew out of the Jewish and Christian apocalyptic tradition, not (as Fascher, $\Pi\rho o\phi\acute{\eta}\tau\eta s$, p. 222) out of Phrygian mystery-religion. Jerome, *Epist.* 41.4, makes Montanus a former eunuch-priest of Cybele; an anonymous document published by Ficker makes him a former priest of Apollo; but we may suspect that both are guessing.

[3] This is Eusebius' date; Epiphanius gives 157, which some have preferred. See Labriolle, *Crise*, pp. 569 ff., and Lawlor's note in his edition of the *Ecclesiastical History*, II, pp. 180 f.

Montanus. It said: 'I am the Lord God Almighty dwell-
ing at this moment within a man'; and again, 'It is no
angel that is here, nor a human spokesman, but the Lord,
God the Father'. And the voice further explained how
this could be: 'Look,' it said, 'man is like a lyre, and I play
upon him like the plectrum: while the human being
sleeps, I am awake. Look, it is the Lord, who takes away
the hearts of men and puts in them other hearts.'[1] Montanus was not, of course, claiming to be God, any more
than a modern medium claims to be Confucius or
Frederic Myers; it was the alien voice which made the
claim. And it made it in traditional terms: both Athenagoras and the *Cohortatio ad Graecos* use the same musical
simile.[2] A little later the voice began to speak through
two female mediums, Priscilla and Maximilla: prophesy is
infectious. Its utterances were taken down in writing, and
the faithful held that they constituted a Third Testament.

Of this Third Testament only a few scraps have been
preserved, and like most communications from the Beyond these scraps, it must be confessed, are extremely
disappointing. It may be that hostile critics like Epiphanius did not choose the most edifying bits to quote;
but we should expect Tertullian, a convert to Montanism,
to show us what it was that converted him, and he can
hardly be said to have done so. The principal revelation
was that the New Jerusalem would shortly descend from
the skies and the thousand-year reign of Christ on earth

---

[1] Epiphan., *Haer.*, 48.4 and 11 (Labriolle, *Crise*, pp. 37 ff., 45 ff.). For
καταγινόμενος ἐν ἀνθρώπῳ, cf. Porph. *apud* Firm. Mat., *Err. prof. rel.*, 13
(=*Phil. ex orac.*, p. 111 Wolff) 'Serapis vocatus et intra corpus hominis
conl <oc> atus talia respondit'.

[2] Athenagoras, *Legat.*, 7; [Justin], *Cohort. ad Graecos*, 8.

would begin. Christian prophecy had of course long been linked with millennial hopes: the prophets kept the hopes alive and the hopes kept the prophets alive. But whereas orthodox Christians expected the Heavenly City to appear in Palestine, Montanus' voice maintained with sturdy local patriotism that the appointed place was Pepuza, a remote village in Phrygia, where all good Christians should await it. For the rest, as Professor Greenslade has put it, 'the Holy Spirit seemed to say nothing of any religious or intellectual value to his prophets'.[1] Apparently he contented himself with scolding the Bishops for their laxity and imposing a few additional austerities on the elect; according to Tertullian[2] he interested himself even in such matters as determining the proper length for an unmarried woman's veil. Since women are more often successful 'mediums' than men, it was natural that Montanus should give women more importance than the orthodox allowed them: one prophetess even had a vision of Christ under the form of a woman.[3] But his most striking innovation was, it seems, a practical one: he appears to have been the first to pay regular salaries to his missionaries.[4]

---

[1] S. L. Greenslade, *Schism in the Early Church* (1953), p. 109.

[2] Tert., *De virginibus velandis*, 17.6.

[3] Epiphan., *Haer.*, 49.1 (Labriolle, *Crise*, pp. 86 ff.). Similarly the Gnostic Marcus communicated to his female disciples the gift of prophecy (Iren., *Haer.*, 1.13). Justin, *Dial.*, 88.1, notes that there are female as well as male *prophetai* among the Christians, and in the Phrygian Church there seems to have been a tradition of female prophecy: Eusebius' anti-Montanist source mentions (*Hist. Eccl.*, 5.17.3 f.) a prophetess Ammia of Philadelphia, whom the Montanists claimed as a forerunner, and who must belong to the first half of the second century (cf. W. M. Calder in *Bulletin John Rylands Library*, 7 (1922–3), pp. 329 f.).

[4] Eus., *Hist. Eccl.*, 5.18.2. It would seem from this passage that Montanus, like Cyprian, combined his 'pneumatic' gifts with the talents of a good organiser.

The Bishops, stung by Montanus' criticism and reluctant to admit any further Testaments, responded by excommunicating him and attempting to exorcise the evil spirits which possessed his followers. But Montanism was not easily killed either by the Bishops or by the failure to keep the appointment at Pepuza. From Phrygia it spread throughout the East, and thence to Rome, to North Africa, and even to distant Spain. And although Maximilla had declared, 'After me shall be no more prophets, but the end of the world,'[1] prophecy nevertheless continued. Tertullian knows a woman who 'converses with angels and sometimes even with the Lord' and who has seen a human soul in bodily shape (thus proving to his satisfaction that souls are corporeal). A generation later, Cyprian knows of children who are favoured with visions and auditions sent by the Holy Spirit, not only in sleep but in waking states of *ekstasis*.[2] And we hear also of a Cappadocian prophetess who soon after 235 took it on herself to administer the sacraments, claimed to be able to produce earthquakes, and offered to lead God's people back to Jerusalem: it would seem from Firmilian's account that the renewal of persecution under Maximinus had combined with natural disasters and growing economic hardship to rekindle millennial expectations.[3]

[1] Epiphan., *Haer.*, 48.2 (Labriolle, *Crise*, pp. 68 f.).

[2] Tert., *De anima*, 9; Cyprian, *Epist.* 16.4. Compare the boy-medium employed by Apuleius (*Apol.*, 42). It is possible that something in the North African temperament or cultural tradition was especially favourable to states of dissociation: cf. P. Courcelle, *Les Confessions de Saint Augustin dans la tradition littéraire* (1963), pp. 127–36.

[3] Firmilian *apud* Cyprian, *Epist.* 75.10. Cf. K. Aland, *Z.N.T.W.*, 46 (1955), pp. 110 f. Labriolle argued (*Crise*, p. 487) that this lady cannot have been a Montanist, since her goal was Jerusalem and not Pepuza; but by her time the appointment at Pepuza may have been cancelled (Tertullian never mentions

After the triumph of Constantine such hopes appeared anachronistic, yet Montanism lingered on in its original strongholds throughout the fourth and fifth centuries. Arcadius ordered the Montanist books to be burnt and their assemblies suppressed; but it was not until the reign of Justinian that the last Montanists locked themselves into their churches and burned themselves to death rather than fall into the hands of their fellow-Christians.[1]

The eventual defeat of Montanism was inevitable. It is already foreshadowed in the sage advice whispered by the Holy Spirit to Ignatius: 'Do nothing without the Bishop.'[2] In vain did Tertullian protest that the Church is not a collection of Bishops; in vain did Irenaeus plead against the expulsion of prophecy.[3] From the point of view of the hierarchy the Third Person of the Trinity had out-lived his primitive function.[4] He was too deeply en-

---

it).—The effect of persecution in stimulating millennial expectations was noticed by Eusebius, *Hist. Eccl.*, 6.7. It is surprising that the disastrous third century did not produce more violent chiliastic movements; one must suppose that ecclesiastical control was already fairly strict and efficient. For such movements at a somewhat earlier date see Hippolytus, *In Dan.*, 4.18 f.

[1] *Cod. Theod.*, 16.5.48; Procopius, *Hist. arc.*, 11.14.21. Cf. Labriolle, *Crise*, pp. 528–36.

[2] Ignat., *Philad.*, 7; cf. *Magn.*, 6, where we are told that 'the Bishop presides in place of God'. Ignatius was, of course, himself a Bishop.

[3] Tert., *De pudicitia*, 21; Iren., *Haer.*, 3.11.12. On the decline of prophecy see Fascher, Προφήτης, pp. 220 f., and H. Lietzmann, *The Founding of the Church Universal* (Eng. trans., 1950), pp. 56–9.

[4] Origen attempted—for quite other reasons, it is true—to reduce the Holy Ghost to the rank of a subordinate agent (*Princ.*, 1.3.5), but his view was not accepted by the Church. The Apologists have little to say about the Third Person, whom they tend to identify with the Second (Lietzmann, *op. cit.*, p. 210); and St Basil later writes that as regards the nature of the Holy Ghost the least 'dangerous' course is to admit one's ignorance (*Contra Sab. et Ar.*, 6, P.G. 31, 613 A). I am disposed to agree with Edwyn Bevan (*Symbolism and Belief*, p. 191), against Reitzenstein, Leisegang and others, that initially this personification of a psychological state was 'an attempt to explain an actual

trenched in the New Testament to be demoted, but he ceased in practice to play any audible part in the counsels of the Church. The old tradition of the inspired *prophetes* who spoke what came to him was replaced by the more convenient idea of a continuous divine guidance which was granted, without their noticing it, to the principal Church dignitaries. Prophecy went underground, to re-appear in the chiliastic manias of the later Middle Ages[1] and in many subsequent evangelical movements: John Wesley was to recognise a kindred spirit in Montanus, whom he judged to be 'one of the holiest men in the second century'.[2] With that epitaph we may leave him.

experience'. Initially God the Holy Ghost was God the Invader, but he kept his independent status long after the recurrence of his invasions had ceased to be acceptable to the Church.

[1] See Norman Cohn's fascinating book, *The Pursuit of the Millennium*. It is worth adding that one specialised function anciently discharged by the *prophetai* survived in the Order of Exorcists, who are listed among the clergy of the Roman Church about the middle of the third century (Eus., *Hist. Eccl.*, 6.43. 11).

[2] John Wesley, *Sermons*, ed. Jackson, II, p. 328, quoted by Labriolle, *Crise*, p. 129.

CHAPTER III

MAN AND THE DIVINE WORLD

I have run round the world of variety, and am now centered in eternity; that is the womb out of which I was taken, and to which my desires are now reduced.

JACOB BAUTHUMLEY

THE experiences I discussed in chapter II were border-line experiences: their religious status is ambiguous—that is why I called them 'daemonic'. In our culture visions and voices are commonly treated as symptoms of illness; and dreams are regarded as a channel of communication not between God and man but between the unconscious and the conscious parts of the human psyche. Phenomena of this sort still play an important rôle in the religious life of certain individuals and certain sects, but most of us are inclined to dismiss them as belonging at best to the pathology of religion. I now propose to exemplify and discuss a class of experiences whose nature is indeed obscure and ill-defined but whose religious character and religious importance is generally admitted.

All the beliefs and experiences to be examined here are of the kind loosely described as 'mystical'. But 'mysticism' is a dangerously vague term. For the purpose of this chapter I shall adopt the strict definition which Lalande gives in his *Vocabulaire de la Philosophie*:[1] mysticism is 'belief in the possibility of an intimate and direct union of the human spirit with the fundamental principle of being, a union which constitutes at once a mode of existence and a mode of knowledge different from and superior to normal existence and knowledge'. Persons who are of the opinion that such union is possible I shall call 'mystical theorists'; persons who believe that they have themselves experienced it I shall call 'practising mystics': the first class of persons of course includes the second, but not *vice versa*. If we define our terms in this way, our first task is to distinguish, so far as we can, specifically mystical theories and experiences from others which can only be called 'mystical' in the loose and not in the precise sense. There is much confusion on this subject in works dealing with the religious phenomena of our period.[2]

One frequent source of confusion is the Greek word *ekstasis*. Since in the literature of medieval mysticism 'ecstasy' is the standard description for the state of mystical union, it is all too easy to read this meaning back into the Greek term. But *ekstasis* and its cognates have in fact

[1] Fifth edition (1947), 644, quoted by Festugière, *Révélation*, IV, p. 265. This definition has the merits (a) of not introducing the term 'God' (which some oriental mystics would certainly reject), (b) of stressing equally the existential and the cognitive aspects of the experience.

[2] E.g. so good a scholar as H.-C. Puech, after rightly remarking that Christian mysticism in the familiar sense was late in emerging, adds that 'it started from a "mysticism" where ecstasy is essentially attached and subordinated to prophecy' (*Rev. d'Hist. et Phil. Rel.* (1933), p. 513). This states the historical sequence correctly, but fails to make clear that the 'ecstasy' of the prophet is a quite different *psychological* state from the 'ecstasy' of mystical union. And even Nilsson can couple the 'stille Ekstase' of Plotinus with the alleged levitation of Iamblichus as if these were phenomena of the same order (*Gesch.*, II, p. 415).

a very wide range of application.[1] In classical Greek they
are used to describe any departure from the normal condition, any abrupt change of mind or mood, and out of
this usage various more specialised senses developed.
They can denote a state of awe or stupefaction, as when
Jesus disputed with the doctors and the onlookers *exis-
tanto*, 'were astonished'.[2] They can denote hysteria or in-
sanity, as they regularly do in Aristotle and in the medical
writers.[3] And they can denote possession, whether divine
(as in the case of the Old Testament prophets) or diabolic
(as in the *ekstasis* which Origen attributes to the Pythia[4]):
this usage is common from Philo onwards. In none of
these senses has *ekstasis* anything to do with mystical
union. The *ekstasis* which Philo ascribes to the Hebrew
prophets has sometimes been confused with it, quite
wrongly, as is clear from Philo's account of such *ekstasis*.
'The mind in us', he says, 'is banished from its house upon
the coming of the divine spirit, and upon its withdrawal
is again restored; for mortal and immortal may not share
the same house.'[5] This is not a description of mystical

[1] Cf. Pfister in *Pisciculi F. J. Doelger* (1939), pp. 178 ff., and in *R.A.C.*, s.v.
Ekstase; also *Pat. Lex.*, s.v. ἔκστασις. Various senses were already distinguished
by Philo, *Quis rer.*, 249.

[2] Luke ii. 47. Cf. Plato, *Menex.*, 235 A 7, Menander, fr. 136 Koerte τὰ
μηδὲ προσδοκῶμεν' ἔκστασιν φέρει, etc.

[3] Ar., *E.N.*, 1149 b 35 ἐξέστηκε τῆς φύσεως ὥσπερ οἱ μαινόμενοι,
Hipp., *Prorrh.*, 2.9, αἱ . . . μελαγχολικαὶ αὗται ἐκστάσιες οὐ λυσιτελέες,
etc.

[4] Origen, *c. Cels.*, 7.3. This pejorative sense is the usual one in Origen
(W. Völker, *Das Vollkommenheitsideal des O.* (1931), pp. 137 ff.). The single
instance of a 'mystical' use of ἔκστασις in Origen which Völker claimed to
have found, at *Hom. in Num.*, 27.12, appears to me extremely doubtful.

[5] Philo, *Quis rer.*, 264 f. Much of his language is 'mystical' in the loose sense
of the term, but the only quasi-mystical experience which Philo claims per-
sonally to have enjoyed is the 'inspiration' of the writer when ideas flow un-
bidden to his pen (*Migr. Abr.*, 7).

union; what it describes is a state of temporary 'possession' or what is nowadays called 'trance-mediumship'. It is the supernatural spirit which descends into a human body, not the man who raises himself or is raised above the body. So far as I know, the earliest application of the word to mystical experience in the strict sense is in a famous sentence of Plotinus,[1] where mystical union is described as 'an *ekstasis*, a simplification and surrender[2] of the self, an aspiration towards contact which is at once a stillness and a mental effort of adaptation'.[3] It is apparently from Plotinus, through Gregory of Nyssa, that Christian mysticism derived this use of the term *ekstasis*.

Let me give another example of the deceptiveness of words. The formula 'I am Thou and Thou art I' has often been used by Christian, Indian and Moslem mystics to express the identity of the soul with its divine ground: for example Angela of Foligno in the thirteenth century thought that she heard Christ say to her, 'Thou art I and I am Thou'.[4] Now there are half a dozen instances of this formula of reciprocal identity being used in or about our period; but it would be rash to assume that it was used in Angela's sense. Thus we read in a magical papyrus an invocation to the supreme god of the cosmos to enter into the magician 'for all the days of his life' and to execute

[1] Plot., VI, ix, 11.22 Br. At V, iii, 7.14 and VI, vii, 17.40 the word has its ordinary broad sense of departure from one's original condition.

[2] ἐπίδοσις is usually so understood here: for the thought, cf. V, v, 8.11. A possible alternative rendering is 'expansion': cf. Ar., *De anima*, 417 b 7.

[3] I understand ἐφαρμογή as the 'fitting' of the soul's centre to the great Centre (VI, ix, 8.19): cf. VI, ii, 8.30.

[4] I have taken this and most of the following examples from O. Weinreich's paper in *Arch. f. Rel.*, 19 (1918), pp. 165 ff.

'all the wishes of his soul', after which the magician declares 'for Thou art I and I am Thou: whatever I say must come to pass'.[1] Plainly here there is no question of mystical union: the reciprocal identity has been magically induced by the preceding incantations; it is to be lifelong; and the magician's motive for inducing it is the acquisition of personal power. The most we can say is that the author may have picked up a formula of religious origin, ascribed magical virtue to it, and utilised it for his own ends: the magical papyri constantly operate with the debris of other people's religion.[2] Much closer, at least in appearance, to Angela's claim is a passage in the Gnostic *Pistis Sophia* where Jesus is made to say of the true Gnostic, 'That man is I and I am that man'.[3] But the most interesting example of the formula occurs in the Ophite *Gospel of Eve*, where a 'voice of thunder' says, 'I am Thou and Thou art I: where thou art, there am I also. I am dispersed in all things: wherever thou wilt, thou dost assemble me, and in assembling me thou dost assemble thyself.'[4] This

[1] *P.G.M.*, xiii, 795. The formula is similarly used at *P.G.M.*, viii, 36 and 50, after an invocation to Hermes to enter into the magician 'as babes enter the womb' (viii, 1). Two other passages where the formula occurs have no relevance to our present topic. In M. Berthelot's *Alchimistes grecs* (1887–8), I, pp. 28 ff., the identification asserted is that of the god Horus with the angel Amnael; in Irenaeus, *Haer.*, 1.13.3, it is that of the Gnostic Marcus with his female disciples, consummated, according to Irenaeus, by sexual union.

[2] Cf. M. P. Nilsson, 'Die Religion in den griech. Zauberpapyri', *Bull. Soc. des Lettres* (*Lund*), 1948, pp. 59 ff.; and A. D. Nock, *J. Egypt. Arch.*, 15 (1929), pp. 219 ff.

[3] *Pistis Sophia*, 96, p. 168 Schmidt. The reference, however, seems to be to an *eventual* absorption of the Gnostic in the Godhead (cf. F. C. Burkitt, *Church and Gnosis*, p. 77).

[4] Epiphanius, *Haer.*, 26.3.1 (=Hennecke, *NT Apokryphen*[3], p. 166). For the pantheistic language cf. *Gospel of Thomas*, saying 77: 'I am the All; from me the All has gone forth, and to me the All has returned. Cleave the wood: I am there. Lift up the stone, and you will find me.'

73

is not the language of Angela, or of Plotinus; but it does seem to be the language of extroverted or pantheistic mysticism. I shall come back to that subject; but I must first discuss another mode of experience which is easily confused with mystical union.

This is the experience described as 'divinisation' (θεὸς γενέσθαι, θεοποιεῖσθαι, (ἀπο)θεωθῆναι). The notion that a human being might become a god or daemon after death had of course long been familiar: it is often asserted on pagan tombstones of the Hellenistic and Roman periods.[1] But that a man should become a god in his lifetime, 'a god walking about in the flesh', as Clement puts it,[2] must seem to us rather odd, if we leave aside the conventions of Hellenistic and Roman ruler-cult. Yet we find this language repeatedly used not only by pagans like Plotinus, Porphyry and the Hermetists, but by Irenaeus and Clement, Origen and Gregory of Nyssa. In order to understand it we should of course remember in the first place that in a polytheistic society the word *theos* did not carry the overwhelming overtones of awe and remoteness that the word 'God' carries for us. In popular Greek tradition a god differed from a man chiefly in being exempt from death and in the supernatural power which this exemption conferred on him. Hence the favourite saying that 'Man is a mortal god, and a god an immortal man'; hence also the possibility of mistaking a man for a god if he appears to display supernatural powers, as is said

[1] Cf. R. Lattimore, *Illinois Studies*, 28 (1942), and A.-J. Festugière, *L'idéal rel. des grecs*, 1932, Part II, ch. 5.

[2] Clem., *Strom.*, 7.101.4. Cf. Epicurus, fr. 141, ἄφθαρτός μοι περιπάτει καὶ ἡμᾶς ἀφθάρτους διανοοῦ.

to have happened to Paul and Barnabas at Lystra and on several occasions to Apollonius of Tyana.[1]

The philosophers, however, had added another qualification for being a god—perfect goodness.[2] And man, they said, should imitate this divine goodness so far as in him lay. This is the doctrine of *homoiosis*, 'assimilation to God', first stated by Plato in a famous passage of the *Theaetetus*, and constantly echoed by the Platonists of our period, both pagan and Christian.[3] It is a moral and not a mystical doctrine: assimilation is not identification. It points, however, to identification as an ideal goal, so that Plotinus can say that the ultimate aim of the good man is not the negative one of avoiding sin but the positive one of being a god, and Clement can say that such a man 'practises to be a god'.[4] In passages of this kind 'divinisation' seems to be no more than the theoretical limiting case of assimilation: as such it serves to characterise the ideal sage, who will, as Porphyry puts it, 'divinise himself

[1] Acts xiv. 8 ff.; Philostr., *Vit. Apoll.*, 4.31; 5.24; 7.11. On the limited implications of the term θεός see A. D. Nock, 'Deification and Julian', *J.R.S.*, 41 (1951), pp. 115–23.

[2] Cf. Plut., *Aristides*, 6, 'Deity is held to be distinguished by three characteristics, imperishability, power and virtue'.

[3] Plato, *Theaet.*, 176 B, φυγὴ δὲ ὁμοίωσις θεῷ κατὰ τὸ δυνατόν · ὁμοίωσις δὲ δίκαιον καὶ ὅσιον μετὰ φρονήσεως γενέσθαι. It is significant that in later quotations of Plato's phrase, e.g. in Plotinus, the qualifying words κατὰ τὸ δυνατόν are often omitted. The history of the idea has been carefully traced by H. Merki in his book Ὁμοίωσις Θεῷ (1952).

[4] Plot., I, ii, 6.2 (where we should translate 'to be *a* god' and not, as MacKenna, 'to be God': cf. line 6); Clem., *Strom.*, 6.113.3. On 'divinisation' in Clement see G. W. Butterworth, *J.T.S.*, 17 (1916), pp. 157–69; in the Greek Fathers generally, J. Gross, *La Divinisation des chrétiens d'après les pères grecs* (1938). Butterworth says of Clement that 'what his hyperbolical language means is simply this, that the divine element in man is gradually brought into closer and more conscious union with God from whom in the beginning it came' (*loc. cit.*, p. 160). This is perhaps too sweeping a reduction; it does not allow for the influence of Gnostic thought on Clement.

by his likeness to God'.¹ It is presumably in this sense that orthodox Catholic theologians could speak of 'divinisation'. They were able to find biblical authority for the idea in Genesis i. 26 and in Psalms lxxxii. 6.

But there are other passages, both pagan and Christian, where these expressions seem to denote an actual change of identity, the substitution of a divine for a human personality, brought about either by a magical ritual or by an act of divine grace or by some combination of the two. As Festugière has shown,² this is clearly the meaning of the thirteenth Hermetic tract: it describes an experience of *regeneration* whereby a living man becomes 'a god and the son of God, all in all, composite of all the divine powers' which have entered into him.³ This is nothing less than an actual invasion of man by God: as such, it is comparable to Philo's *ekstasis* and to the cases of divine possession we examined in chapter II, but it differs from them in that the resulting state is permanent. That the reborn are henceforth sinless is the teaching both of the Hermetist and of Clement.⁴ For the Hermetist 'regeneration' seems to depend partly on a ritual act,⁵ accompanied by com-

---

¹ Porph., *Ad Marc.*, 285.20 Nauck. Cf. Porph. *apud* Aug., *Civ. Dei*, 19.23, 'Imitation divinises us by bringing us nearer to God'.

² *Révélation*, IV, pp. 200–67.

³ *Corp. Herm.*, xiii, 2.

⁴ But not of Origen, who took the wiser view that as the soul is never incapable of redemption, so it is never incapable of lapsing into sin: the freedom to choose is part of its inalienable nature. Biblical authority for the doctrine of the 'sinless' Gnostic was, however, found in 1 John iii. 6.

⁵ The candidate for divinisation has to 'draw in' (ἐπισπάσασθαι) the divine breath (*Corp. Herm.*, xiii, 7), just as the candidate for immortality has to do in *P.G.M.*, iv, 537: in both cases the *pneuma* is conceived in material terms. Cf. Festugière, *Révélation*, III, p. 171 and IV, p. 249; and the early-nineteenth-century account of a 'conversion' quoted by William James, *Varieties*, Lecture

munication of occult knowledge, and partly on divine grace; for Clement it depends on baptism plus education plus grace; some Christian Gnostics held that it required a special rite, a second baptism, others that the acquisition of *gnosis* was enough by itself.[1] In all these cases the underlying psychological fact appears to be the phenomenon of conversion, carrying with it the conviction that the slate has been wiped clean and the magical disappearance—at least for the time being—of the desire to sin.[2] Where the conversion is sudden and complete, the subject feels himself raised to a new level of existence: as Lifton has expressed it, a major change in ideology demands a major change in identity.[3] We noticed in the last chapter some indications suggesting a crisis of identity: 'Is this an image of Aristides or an image of Asclepius?' 'Is this the voice

ix: 'there was a stream (resembling air in feeling) came into my mouth and heart in a more sensible manner than that of drinking anything, which continued, as near as I could judge, five minutes or more'.

[1] Irenaeus, *Haer.*, 1.21.1 (Marcosians). For the magical effects of baptism cf. Cyprian, *Ad Donatum* (*De gratia Dei*), 3–4: on being baptised 'in a wonderful way the doubtful suddenly became certain, the closed open, the dark light, and what had been thought impossible became possible'.

[2] Cf. Kirk, *Vision*, pp. 229–34. Since, in the words of Ignatius, 'the spiritual man cannot do what is fleshly', some concluded that if he appeared to do what is fleshly he was not really doing it. Certain Gnostics are accused by the orthodox Fathers of disregarding all moral rules on this basis. On such matters the Fathers are not the most reliable witnesses, but their charges receive support from the independent testimony of Plotinus, II, ix, 15, as well as from what has happened in other cultures (cf. Zaehner, *Mysticism*, pp. 187 f., 206).

[3] R. J. Lifton, *Thought Reform and the Psychology of Totalism* (1961), pp. 454 ff. The problem of personal identity is explicitly raised and discussed in two passages of Plotinus: VI, iv, 14.16 ff. and I, i,10 f.: is the ego ($\dot{\eta}\mu\epsilon\hat{\iota}s$) to be equated with the timeless Self which is part of the structure of Reality, or with 'that other man who desired to exist and found the Self and attached himself to it'? His answer is that the identity of the ego is unstable: its boundaries fluctuate with the fluctuations of consciousness. The significance of this discovery is well brought out in the recent book of P. Hadot, *Plotin ou la simplicité du regard* (1963), ch. ii.

of Montanus or the Voice that uses Montanus?' Similarly a man could ask, 'Am I still the insecure and sinful being that I was yesterday? Am I not rather a new being, reborn into security and sinlessness?' And, in Freudian terms, such a man could resolve his crisis by introjecting the potent father-image. Henceforth he could pray, as the Adamites did, to 'Our Father which art *in us*'.[1]

It should be clear that the phenomenon I have been discussing is entirely distinct from mystical union, an experience of brief duration which as a rule recurs only at long intervals if at all. Plotinus can indeed say that in mystical union the soul 'has become God or rather *is* God';[2] but this is not the sense in which Clement or the Hermetists speak of 'divinisation'. The distinction is well stated by Norman Cohn in relation to late medieval mysticism. After quoting the claim made in the fourteenth-century pamphlet *Schwester Katrei* that 'Christ has made me his equal and I can never lose that condition', Cohn continues: 'The gulf which separates such experiences from those of the great Catholic mystics is of course immense. The *unio mystica* recognised by the Church was a momentary illumination, granted only occasionally, perhaps but once in a lifetime. And whatever energies it might release and whatever assurance it might bestow, the human being who experienced it did not thereby shed his human condition; it was as an ordinary mortal that he had to live out

---

[1] Cohn, *Pursuit of the Millennium*, p. 233. In the vast melting-pot of the later Empire, which flung together men of the most diverse racial, religious and social origins, we should expect the question, 'What am I?' to assume unusual importance, for the same reasons which make it important in modern America: cf. Erik H. Erikson, *Identity and the Life Cycle* (1956).

[2] Plot., VI, ix, 9.59.

his life on earth. The heretical mystic, on the other hand, felt himself to be utterly transformed; he had not merely been united with God, he was identical with God and would remain so for ever.'[1] For 'the great Catholic mystics' read 'Plotinus', for 'the heretical mystic' read 'certain Hermetists and Christian Gnostics', and the distinction applies perfectly to our period. Plotinus also rejected firmly the megalomaniac claim of the Gnostics to a monopoly of the divine presence. For him God is present to all beings, and the power of becoming aware of that presence is a capacity 'which all men possess, though few use it' (I, vi, 8.24). 'If God is not in the world', he tells the Gnostics, 'then neither is he in you, and you can have nothing to say about him' (II, ix, 16.25).

I turn now to the difficult subject of mystical union proper. Here too there are distinctions to be drawn. In two important recent books, Professor Zaehner's *Mysticism Sacred and Profane* and Professor Stace's *Mysticism and Philosophy*, an attempt has been made to establish a morphology of mysticism. The two authors use different terms and reach different conclusions, but they are agreed in distinguishing two main types of experience, extrovertive (called by Zaehner 'nature mysticism') and introvertive. I quote Stace's definitions.

> The extrovertive experience looks outward through the senses, while the introvertive looks inward into the mind. Both culminate in the perception of an ultimate unity with which the perceiver realises his own union or even identity. But the extrovertive mystic, using his physical senses, perceives the multiplicity of external material objects mystically transfigured so that the One, or the Unity, shines through them. The introvertive mystic, on

[1] Cohn, *Pursuit of the Millennium*, p. 184.

the contrary, seeks by deliberately shutting off the senses . . . to plunge into the depths of his own ego.[1]

Thus far Stace. In which of these two modes a man may find unity is, I suppose, in part a matter of individual temperament and in part culturally determined. And from what I said in chapter 1 it will be evident that the central tendencies of our period favoured an introvertive rather than an extrovertive approach. The current of 'cosmic optimism', the feeling of awe in the presence of the visible cosmos, which springs from the *Timaeus* and flows deep or shallow in all the Stoics, was beginning to run into the sands, though it never wholly vanished, while the opposite current of 'cosmic pessimism' gained steadily in strength. The old feeling of the divinely ordered unity of things is still alive and powerful in Marcus Aurelius, as where he speaks of 'one world containing all, one God penetrating all, one substance and one law'. And he reminds himself of his own unity with it: 'every man's mind is a god and an emanation from deity'; the man who cuts himself off from the City of God is like a rebellious cancer on the face of Nature.[2] But these are tradi-

---

[1] Stace, *Mysticism and Philosophy*, pp. 61–2 (slightly shortened). Zaehner, *Mysticism*, p. 50, defines 'natural mystical experience' as 'an experience of Nature in all things or of all things as being one'. He rightly objects to the term 'pantheistic mysticism', since some mystics (notably Richard Jefferies) have recognised nothing in the experience which they are prepared to call 'God'. Others may object to the term 'extrovertive' on the ground that the experience is really a projection of the inner world upon the outer, not a straightforward receptivity to sensory impressions. But at least it involves the use of the senses, which 'introvertive' mysticism excludes. A comparable distinction between 'Einheitsschau' (extrovertive) and 'Selbstversenkung' (introvertive) had already been drawn by Rudolf Otto, *Mysticism East and West* (Eng. trans., 1932), ch. iv.

[2] M. Ant., 7.9; 12.26; 4.29. These and other passages, though traditional in substance, seem to me to be deeply felt (cf. p. 8, n. 1). William James hardly did justice to their warmth when he spoke of 'a frosty chill about his

tional thoughts; there is nothing to indicate personal mystical experience. More characteristic of the time is his repeated stress on the need for withdrawal into the inner life, 'the little domain that is the self'. 'Dig within', he says; 'within is the fountain of good which is always ready to bubble up so long as you continue digging.' And once he exclaims triumphantly, 'Today I have escaped all circumstance, or rather, I have expelled all circumstance; for it was not outside me but inside me in my thoughts.'[1] Sayings like these point forward in some degree to Plotinus: while Marcus' outer man wages efficient war against the Sarmatians, his inner man is engaged upon a journey into the interior. Yet I should hesitate to call him even a 'mystical theorist'. His concern is simply to liberate himself from emotional attachment to the external world. Marcus can say 'The fountain of good is within', but not yet with Plotinus 'All things are within'. The external world, however repugnant, is still solid and opaque to him.

More suggestive of the extrovertive kind of mystical experience is the passage I quoted from the Gnostic

words which you rarely find in a Jewish and never in a Christian piece of religious writing' (*Varieties*, Lecture ii). Wilamowitz was nearer the truth when he observed that Marcus had both faith and charity: what he lacked was hope ('Kaiser Marcus', *Vortrag* (1931), p. 10).

[1] M. Ant., 4.3.4; 7.59; 9.13; cf. also 6.11, ἐπάνιθι εἰς ἑαυτόν. On the general topic of withdrawal (ἀναχώρησις) into the self see Festugière, *Personal Religion*, pp. 58 ff.; on the special term ἐπιστρέφεσθαι εἰς (πρὸς, ἐπὶ) ἑαυτόν, P. Aubin, *Le Problème de la 'Conversion'* (1963). This latter phrase is used once by Marcus (9.42.4: cf. 8.48 εἰς ἑαυτὸ συστραφέν, of the ἡγεμονικόν), and several times by Epictetus, but without the metaphysical overtones which it acquires in Plotinus: see my note on Proclus, *Elements of Theology*, props. 15–17. It is interesting that Aubin could find no instance of ἐπιστρέφεσθαι εἰς ἑαυτόν in Christian writers earlier than Plotinus (Origen, *Comm. in Gen.*, 3.9, is no real exception).

Gospel of Eve. And I will put beside it one from the eleventh Hermetic tract where Nous says to Hermes,

> If you do not make yourself equal to God, you cannot apprehend God, for like is apprehended by like.[1] Outleap all body and expand yourself to the unmeasured greatness; outstrip all time and become Eternity:[2] so shall you apprehend God. . . . Embrace in yourself all sensations of all created things, of fire and water, dry and wet; be simultaneously everywhere, on sea and land and in the sky; be at once unborn and in the womb, young and old, dead and beyond death; and if you can hold all these things together in your thought, times and places and substances, qualities and quantities, then you can apprehend God. But if you abase your soul by shutting it up in its body, if you say 'I understand nothing, I can do nothing; I am afraid of the sea, I cannot climb the sky; I do not know what I have been, I do not know what I shall be', in that case what have you to do with God?[3]

Is this just a piece of rhetorical rodomontade, or is it a serious exercise in what the Germans call 'Einfühlung'—in fact, an exercise in extrovertive mysticism? Has the writer known an experience like that described by the Ulster novelist Forrest Reid, in which 'it was as if every-

---

[1] Plotinus applies the same traditional principle to mystical union, VI, ix, 11. 32. For its history see Schneider, *Der Gedanke der Erkenntnis des Gleichen durch Gleiches in ant. u. patr. Zeit.*

[2] *Αἰὼν γενοῦ.* On the interpretation of this sentence (which admits of two punctuations) see Festugière, *Révélation*, IV, pp. 148 f.; and on the various meanings attached to αἰών in later antiquity, Nock, *Harv. Theol. Rev.* 27 (1934), pp. 78–99, and Festugière, *Révélation*, IV, chs. viii and ix. Cf. the 'sensation of eternity' described by Freud's anonymous friend (*Civilization and its Discontents*, p. 2, Eng. trans.). However, an 'ascent to *aion*' need be no more than a rhetorical metaphor for philosophical understanding, as in fr. 37 of the Epicurean Metrodorus (=Clem., *Strom.*, 5.138) ἀναβὰς τῇ ψυχῇ ἕως ἐπὶ τὸν αἰῶνα καὶ τὴν ἀπειρίαν τῶν πραγμάτων κατεῖδες καὶ "τά τ' ἐσσόμενα πρό τ' ἐόντα".

[3] *Corp. Herm.*, xi, 20. Cf. xiii, 11, where the initiate claims to have achieved this experience of union with all Nature by the 'intellectual energy which he has obtained from the Powers'.

thing that had seemed to be external and around me were suddenly within me. The whole world seemed to be within me. It was within me that the trees waved their green branches, it was within me that the skylark was singing, it was within me that the hot sun shone, and that the shade was cool'?[1] Is that the sort of thing the Hermetist has in mind? I have no firm answer to give. I can only say as Festugière does at the end of his great work on the *Hermetica*, 'the historian knows only what he is told; he cannot penetrate the secrets of the heart'.[2]

But it is in any case instructive to compare this Hermetic passage with an exercise prescribed by Plotinus. Plotinus says:

> Let every soul meditate on this: that she it is who created all things living, breathing into them their principle of life; all that the land breeds or the sea, all creatures of the air and the divine stars in the heaven, she created; the sun she created, and this great firmament was made by her; none other than she apparelled it with order, none other than she revolves it in its appointed courses; yet is soul a kind distinct from all that she apparels and moves and makes to live.[3]

Both passages are inspired by the same feeling of the unity of all life; both assert the paradox of the infinitely expansible self. But where the Hermetist is content to equate the self with Nature in all its aspects, Plotinus equates it with the causative force behind Nature. Nor is this all: what for the Hermetist is the final achievement is for Plotinus only the beginning of the ascent. From the contemplation of Nature we must pass to the contemplation

---

[1] Forrest Reid, *Following Darkness*, p. 42, quoted by Zaehner, *Mysticism*, ch. iii.

[2] *Révélation*, IV, p. 267.

[3] Plot., v, i, 2.1 ff.

of the 'intelligible cosmos', the network of pure relations which is mirrored in the self of every man.[1] And at the heart of this network we must discover 'the still point of the turning world', the innermost self which is potentially identical with that nameless reservoir of force called by Plotinus the One, or the Good, or sometimes God. For Plotinus the soul's journey is a voyage of self-discovery: 'It shall come', he says, 'not to another but to itself.' *Panta eiso* is his motto, 'the sum of things is within us':[2] if we wish to know the Real, we have only to look in ourselves. In other words, he is the perfect type of the introvertive mystic.

He is also, with his pupil Porphyry, the only person of our period who is stated in so many words to have enjoyed mystical union. Four times, according to Porphyry, in the six years that the two men worked together 'Plotinus lifted himself to the primal and transcendent God by meditation and by the methods Plato indicated in the *Symposium*'; Porphyry himself had attained the same goal but once, many years later.[3] And we have the testimony of Plotinus himself in the unique autobiographical passage where he speaks of occasions when 'I awakened out of the body into myself and came to be external to all other things and contained within myself, when I saw a marvellous beauty and was confident, then if ever, that I belonged to the higher order, when I actively enjoyed the noblest form of life, when I had become one with the

---

[1] Plot., III, iv, 3.22, ἐσμὲν ἕκαστος κόσμος νοητός. I think it would be true to say that for Plotinus this world of Platonic Forms is already the object of a kind of mystical experience.

[2] Plot., VI, ix, 11.38; III, viii, 6.40.

[3] Porph., *Vit. Plot.*, 23.7 ff.

Divine and stabilised myself in the Divine.'[1] Elsewhere
Plotinus has described in memorable prose, if not the
mystical union itself, at any rate the steps which lead up
to it. He tells us that when we have achieved through intellectual and moral self-training the right disposition,
we must practise a discipline of negation: we must think
away the corporeal opaqueness of the world, think away
the spatio-temporal frame of reference, and at last think
away even the inner network of relations. What is left?
Nothing, it would seem, but a centre of awareness which
is potentially, but not yet actually, the Absolute.[2]

The last stage of the experience comes by no conscious
act of will: 'we must wait quietly for its appearance', says
Plotinus, 'and prepare ourselves to contemplate it, as the
eye waits for the sunrise.'[3] But what then happens cannot properly be described in terms of vision, or of any
normal cognitive act;[4] for the distinction of subject and
object vanishes. I quote one of Plotinus' attempts at
description:

> The soul sees God[5] suddenly appearing within it, because there
> is nothing between: they are no longer two, but one; while the
> presence lasts, you cannot distinguish them. It is that union

[1] Plot., IV, viii, 1.1 ff. Elsewhere he appeals to the testimony of 'those who
have had the experience' (I, vi, 7.2; V, v, 8.25; VI, ix, 9.39).

[2] Cf. Plot., VI, viii, 21.25 ff. and VI, ix, 6 f. Passages dealing with mystical
union are collected and analysed in Arnou's book, *Le Désir de Dieu dans la
philosophie de Plotin* (1921). For a penetrating discussion see H.-C. Puech,
Bull. Ass. Budé, 61 (1938), pp. 13–46. Philip Merlan's *Monopsychism, Mysticism, Metaconsciousness: Problems of the soul in the Neoaristotelian and Neoplatonic
tradition* (1963) reached me too late to be used in preparing this chapter, as did
also the brilliant short book of Pierre Hadot, *Plotin ou la simplicité du regard*
(1963).

[3] Plot., V, v, 8.3.

[4] Cf. Plot., V, iii, 14.1 ff.; VI, vii, 35.42 ff.

[5] With the masc. participle φανέντα we must understand, as often in
Plotinus, τὸν θεόν: cf. Schwyzer in *P.-W.*, s.v. Plotinos, col. 515.

which earthly lovers imitate when they would be one flesh. The soul is no longer conscious of being in a body, or of itself as having identity—man or living being, thing or sum of things. . . . For who it is that sees it has no leisure to see. When in this state the soul would exchange its present condition for nothing in the world, though it were offered the kingdom of all the heavens: for this is the Good, and there is nothing better.[1]

This description has many features in common with those which other mystical thinkers have noted at many different times and places. The withdrawal into the self, and the emptying of the self that it may be filled with God; the need for quietness and passivity; the disappearance of the sense of personal identity; the sudden intense and total satisfaction; the awareness that this experience is different in *kind* from any other, and the consequent difficulty in communicating it—all these have been described again and again, from ancient India to modern America, and in much the same terms. In my view it is recognisably the same psychological experience everywhere, however different the glosses that have been put upon it, however incompatible the theologies which it has been held to confirm.

What is distinctively Plotinian—perhaps we should say, distinctively Hellenic—in the mysticism of Plotinus is not the experience itself but his approach to it and his interpretation of it. His approach is severely intellectual, not physiological as in some oriental sects or sacramental as with some Christian mystics. He prescribes no breathing exercises, no navel-brooding, no hypnotic repetition of sacred syllables; and no ritual is needed to provoke the experience. In the purely mental exercises which he does

[1] Plot. VI, vii, 34.12 ff. Cf. also VI, ix, 10-11.

occasionally recommend[1] he relies on the three traditional approaches to the knowledge of God which were
already listed by Albinus a century earlier—the way of
negation (perhaps originally Pythagorean), the way of
analogy (based on Plato's analogy of the sun and the
Good), and the way of eminence (based on the ascent to
absolute Beauty in Plato's *Symposium*).[2] If we can believe
Porphyry, it was by the last of these ways that Plotinus
achieved his personal experience of union; but in his
teaching he also makes free use of the other two.[3] As I
have remarked elsewhere, Plotinus would not have
agreed with Aldous Huxley that 'the habit of analytical thought is fatal to the intuitions of integral thinking'.[4]
On the contrary, the habit of analytical thought is to
Plotinus a necessary and valuable discipline, a *katharsis* in
which the mind must be exercised before it attempts
what Huxley calls 'integral thinking' and Plotinus calls
noesis. For him, as for his master Plato, the contemplative's training should begin with mathematics and
proceed to dialectic:[5] mystical union is not a substitute for
intellectual effort but its crown and goal. Nor is it a
substitute for moral effort, as it may have been in some

[1] E.g. Plot., v, i, 2–3, the passage whose opening words are quoted above, p. 83, and v, viii, 9.

[2] Albinus, *Epitome*, 10, 165.14 ff. Hermann. Cf. appendix I in my edition of Proclus' *Elements of Theology*, pp. 312 f.

[3] Porph., *Vit. Plot.*, 23.9. The Three Ways are briefly referred to by Plotinus at VI, vii, 36.6. His earliest 'mystical' essay, I, vi, is largely a meditation on the *Symposium* passage (210 A–212 A). For the analogy of the sun cf. e.g. I, vii, 1.24 ff. and IV, iii, 11; for the 'way of negation', VI, ix, 3.36 ff.; 6.1 ff.

[4] Aldous Huxley, *The Perennial Philosophy* (1946), p. 27. Cf. *J.R.S.*, 50 (1960), p. 7.

[5] Plot., I, iii, 3. According to Porphyry (*Vit. Plot.*, 14.7), Plotinus was him-self well acquainted with geometry, theory of numbers, mechanics, optics and music, though he did not write on these subjects.

of the Gnostic sects: 'without true virtue', he says, 'all talk of God is but words'.[1] He who would attain to the experience must be an artist in morals: 'he must never cease from carving his own image, stripping away all excess and making straight all crookedness', until there is no foreign thing mixed with the pure self to hinder it from unification.[2]

In his interpretation of the experience Plotinus is nearer to some Indian mystics than he is to the orthodox Christian view.[3] In the first place, it is for him a *natural* event, not a supernatural grace, as in Christian and Moslem theory. It has its natural root in the potential identity of the soul with its divine ground, and in the general law that all things tend to revert to their source. It is the actualisation of something which was only waiting to be realised, the momentary revelation of an eternal datum.[4] 'The One', says Plotinus, 'is always present, since it con-

[1] Plot., II, ix, 15.39. Cf. above, p. 77, n. 2.

[2] Plot., I, vi, 9.7 ff. Perhaps adapted from Plato, *Phdr.*, 252 D, though the point there is wholly different—the 'image' is the lover's image of his beloved. The Plotinian passage is closely imitated by Gregory of Nyssa, *P.G.* 44, 541 D ff. and 1069 B: for him the Logos carves the soul into the image of Christ.

[3] Not all Christian mystics have kept within the bounds imposed on them by Catholic orthodoxy. Eckhart, in particular, when he is not defending himself against charges of heresy, often writes in terms indistinguishable from those of Plotinus, as when he says, 'I have maintained ere this and I still maintain that I already possess all that is granted to me in eternity. For God in the fullness of his Godhead dwells eternally in his image—the soul.'

[4] Cf. H.-C. Puech, *Bull. Ass. Budé*, 61 (1938), p. 45. Plotinus was the first writer to recognise that the psyche includes sensations, desires and dispositions of which the ego is normally unconscious (v, i, 12.5; IV, viii, 8.9; IV, iv, 4.7); and he regards mystical experience as an extension of the ego's awareness into this unconscious region (v, i, 12). Modern analysts can be quoted in support. Freud himself wrote in his *New Introductory Lectures* (Eng. trans., 1933): 'Certain practices of the mystics may succeed in upsetting the normal relations between the different regions of the mind, so that, for example, the perceptual system becomes able to grasp relations in the deeper layers of the Ego, and in the Id, which would otherwise be inaccessible to it.' And according to Erich

tains no otherness; but we are present only when we rid ourselves of otherness.' And he adds, 'The One has no desire towards us, to make us its centre; but our desire is towards it, to realise it as our Centre. It is in fact our Centre always, but we do not always fix our eyes upon the Centre.'[1] That is the second distinctive feature in Plotinus' account of mystical union: like all relations between lower and higher in his system, it is *non-reciprocating*, one-sided. The soul experiences longing (*eros*) towards the One, which can be said, like Aristotle's God, to move the world as the object of the world's desire.[2] But the One cannot experience desire, for desire is a mark of incompleteness; the creature, the effect, cannot influence

---

Fromm (*Psychoanalysis and Religion* (1951), p. 101) 'the process of breaking through the confines of one's organised self—the ego—and of getting in touch with the excluded and disassociated parts of oneself, the unconscious, is closely related to the religious experience of breaking down individuation and feeling one with the All'.

[1] Plot., VI, ix, 8.33.

[2] Cf. Plot., VI, vii, 31.17. I cannot agree with Inge's dictum that 'erotic mysticism is no part of Platonism'. Plotinus, like many Christian mystics, makes free use of erotic imagery to describe mystical union, e.g. here and at VI, ix, 9.24 ff. Since it is claimed to be the most intimate and complete of all unions, it is natural to compare it with the union of the sexes. But the 'erotic' tradition in Western mysticism also has literary sources—Plato's *Symposium* and (for Christians) the Song of Songs as interpreted by Origen. Both Plotinus (VI, ix, 9.28) and Origen (*Comm. in Cant.*, *G.C.S.* VIII, 66.29 ff.) make use in this connection of Plato's distinction between Aphrodite Pandemos and Aphrodite Ourania (*Symp.*, 180 D). It is true that the relationship between man and God as conceived by Plato (and by Plotinus) is very different from that implied in the New Testament (cf. most recently W. J. Verdenius, 'Plato and Christianity', *Ratio* 5 (1963), pp. 15–32). Nevertheless it is not easy historically to draw a sharp line between Christian *agape*-mysticism and Platonist *eros*-mysticism: it appears that both in Origen and in Gregory of Nyssa *agape* and *eros* are quite often used interchangeably (see J. M. Rist's forthcoming book, *Eros and Psyche;* and J. Daniélou, *Platonisme et théologie mystique* (1944), p. 218), and both are influenced in their conception of *eros* by the *Symposium*. Cf. John Burnaby, *Amor Dei* (1938), pp. 15 ff., and A. H. Armstrong's valuable paper, 'Platonic *Eros* and Christian *Agape*', *Downside Review*, 1961, pp. 105 ff.

its cause. Plotinus assures us in so many words that the One has no need of its products and would not care if it had *no* products.[1] He can indeed call it Eros, but only in the sense of being *amor sui*.[2] If we can speak at all of anything like 'grace' in Plotinus, it is only in the sense of a permanent presence of the Divine in all men, a presence which can on rare occasions be consciously experienced by a few men through their own unaided efforts. This is surely quite different from the notion of individual acts of grace which we meet not only in Christian theology but in many pagan writers.[3] But it is, I repeat, a difference of interpretation. I can see no reason to suppose, as certain Catholic writers do, that it implies a totally different psychological experience. When Professor Zaehner, for example, tells me that whereas the monistic mystic 'achieves liberation entirely by his own efforts, in the case of the theistic mystic it is always God who takes the first step', I cannot but suspect that he is reading back into the experience what is in fact a theological gloss on it.[4]

This is not the place in which to examine the sources of

---

[1] Plot., v, v, 12.40–9. The One might say, as Krishna says in the *Bhagavad Gita* (9.29), 'I am indifferent to all generated beings; there is none whom I hate, none whom I love. But they that worship me with devotion dwell in me and I in them.' Marcion seems to have held a similar view of the First God: he is credited with saying 'There is one good God, a single First Principle, a single nameless Power; this one God and single Principle has no concern for the things which happen here in this world' (Epiphanius, *Haer.*, 44.1).

[2] Plot., vi, viii, 15.1.

[3] The idea of divine grace towards the individual is implied in all the pagan aretalogies; it is constantly present in Aelius Aristides and in Apuleius' account of the conversion of Lucius; it occurs also in many of the Hermetists (Festugière, *Révélation*, iii, p. 106), and can be found even in Stoics (cf. Marcus Aurelius on prayer, 9.40). I do not know why some Catholic writers speak as if it were a feature peculiar to Christianity.

[4] Zaehner, *Mysticism*, p. 192 (cf. p. 204). Stace, *Mysticism and Philosophy*, p. 36, takes the same view as I do. Cf. Edwyn Bevan, *Symbolism and Belief*,

Plotinus' characteristic theology or to estimate its religious value. It must suffice to say that he thought he had authority for it in Plato, and that in fact most of its elements are to be found dispersed in the writings of second-century Platonists, though not yet built into a coherent system.[1] It is more relevant to my present purpose to ask whether Plotinus' mystical experience was an isolated phenomenon, the accidental product of an exceptional personality-structure,[2] or whether indications of a tendency to introvertive mysticism are to be found in writers of our period who were independent of Plotinus. In seeking an answer we should remember that mystical experience is not an all-or-none affair; it admits wide variations of intensity and completeness.[3] That being so, it seems justifiable to point in the first place to the new importance attached in Middle-Platonist speculation to the personal quest for God.

pp. 353 f.: 'In most cases where a man tells us that he apprehends something directly, we recognise that he does apprehend something, but it does not follow that he apprehends precisely what he thinks he does. He interprets his actual apprehension by a mass of ideas already in his mind, and the resulting belief may be an amalgam in which, while one constituent is an apprehension of reality, there may also be a large admixture of false imagination.'

[1] See the papers and discussions in *Les Sources de Plotin*.

[2] Freud would, I suspect, have been interested in the one biographical detail of Plotinus' childhood which has been preserved to us, viz. that he refused to be completely weaned until his eighth year (Porph., *Vit. Plot.*, 3.1 ff.). The time of weaning varies widely in different cultures (see Harder's note *ad loc.*); but so prolonged a refusal to grow up would seem to be significant. It would fit Freud's suggestion that mystical experience, with its sense of infinite extension and oneness with the Real, may represent a persistence of infantile feeling in which no distinction is yet drawn between 'self' and 'other', a feeling which 'could co-exist as a sort of counterpart with the narrower and more sharply outlined ego-feeling of maturity' (*Civilization and its Discontents*, Eng. trans., pp. 13 f.).

[3] See the examples of marginal, 'semi-mystical' experiences quoted by Stace, *Mysticism and Philosophy*, ch. ii.

There is a well-known testimony to this in Justin's *Dia: logue with Trypho*, where the author describes such a quest-after seeking in vain to learn about God from a Stoic, an Aristotelian and a Pythagorean, he finally attends the lectures of a Platonist, who at least gives him the hope of seeing God face to face, 'for this', he says, 'is the aim of the philosophy of Plato'.[1] And it seems to have been in fact the Platonists of Justin's time who elaborated the doctrine of the Three Ways to the knowledge of God which I mentioned just now—the doctrine that was later taken over into the philosophy of medieval Christendom. We meet it not only in the systematiser Albinus but with a different terminology in Celsus,[2] and it is expounded in a more popular form by Maximus of Tyre.[3] To the man in the street the term 'philosophy' came increasingly to *mean* the quest for God: as the author of the Hermetic *Asclepius* expresses it, 'philosophy consists solely in learning to know the Deity by habitual contemplation and pious devotion'.[4] And in Maximus we can see what already looks like an established tradition of exercises in introvertive contemplation. We are to 'stop our ears and convert our vision and our other senses inwards upon the self'; this will enable us to mount on the wings of true

[1] Justin, *Dial.*, 2.3–6. The pagan cults and mysteries of our period similarly reflect the longing for personal illumination: cf. Nock, *Conversion*, ch. vii.

[2] Celsus *apud* Orig., *c. Cels.*, 7.42, ἢ τῇ συνθέσει τῇ ἐπὶ τὰ ἄλλα ἢ ἀναλύσει ἀπ' αὐτῶν ἢ ἀναλογίᾳ, where σύνθεσις seems to correspond to the *via eminentiae* and ἀνάλυσις to the *via negationis*: cf. Chadwick *ad loc.* and Festugière, *Révélation*, IV, pp. 119–23. 'The soul', says Celsus elsewhere, 'should be always directed towards God' (8.49).

[3] Max. Tyr., 11.9–12. He does not give names to the Three Ways, but he describes them in Platonic terms: cf. Festugière, *Révélation*, IV, pp. 111–15.

[4] *Asclep.*, 12 (*Corp. Herm.*, II, 312 Nock–Fest.). The writer adds (14) that 'philosophy' must be kept free from 'importunate intellectual curiosity'. Cf. Antonie Wlosok, *Laktanz und die philosophische Gnosis* (1960), pp. 132–6.

reason and passionate desire (*logos* and *eros*) to a place of peace beyond the skies. 'Strip away the other garments,' says Maximus, 'abolish in thought the preoccupation of the eyes, and in what remains you will see the true object of your longing.'[1]

This sounds very like the language of Plotinus, but it need not be based on personal mystical experience. As Festugière has rightly insisted, it has its doctrinal roots in a mystical interpretation of certain passages in Plato—the teaching of the *Phaedo* about withdrawal, the ascent in the *Symposium*, the *Phaedrus* myth, and the passage in the Seventh Letter about the spark which is kindled in the soul. We can perhaps detect a more personal note in a fragment of Numenius, the second-century Pythagorean whose works were read in Plotinus' school and from whom Plotinus was accused of plagiarising.[2] He compares the contemplative to a watcher in a high place who looks out across an empty sea and suddenly catches sight of a single tiny boat: 'in the same way', he says, 'one must withdraw far from the things of sense and enter into solitary communion with the Good, where is no human being nor any other creature nor body great or small, but only a kind of divine desolation which in truth cannot be

---

[1] Max. Tyr., 11.10 b, 11 e. Similarly in the *Hermetica* knowledge of God is often linked with suppression of sense experience: e.g. x, 5, 'Knowledge of the Good is a divine silence and an inhibition of all the senses'; xiii, 7, 'Arrest the activity of the bodily senses and it will be the birth of deity'.

[2] Porph., *Vit. Plot.*, 14.10; 17.1. The importance of Numenius' influence on Neoplatonism seems now to be increasingly recognised: cf. *Les Sources de Plotin*, pp. 1–24 and 33–61; J. C. M. van Winden, *Calcidius on Matter* (1959), pp. 103–28 and *passim*; P. Merlan, *Philol.*, 106 (1962), pp. 137–45; J. M. Rist, *Mediaeval Studies*, 24 (1962), pp. 173–7. He also influenced Origen: cf. Jerome, *Epist.* 70.3 ff., where Origen is said to have proved the principles of Christianity from Plato, Aristotle, *Numenius* and Cornutus.

spoken of or described, where are the haunts and resorts
and splendours of the Good, and the Good itself at rest in
peace and friendliness, the Sovereign Principle riding
serene above the tides of Being'.[1] As I have tried to show
elsewhere,[2] Plotinus has a good many echoes of this remarkable passage, and I think it is a reasonable assumption
that he understood it as a description of mystical union.
We know that Numenius asserted the 'indistinguishable
identity' of the soul with its divine Grounds (*archai*); he
held 'unambiguously' that every soul in some sense *contains* 'the Intelligible World, the gods and daemons, the
Good, and all the prior kinds of Being'.[3] This is the
theoretical basis of Plotinian mysticism; and if Plotinus
took over the theory from Numenius, it is at least possible that he learned the practice from him too.

I should like in passing to call attention to a curious
link between Plotinus and Jewish mystical thought.
In his earliest writing, the essay *On Beauty*, Plotinus
compares the 'stripping' of the soul in preparation
for mystical union with 'the putting off of former
garments' which must be practised by those who enter
'the holy parts of temples'.[4] Commentators have not
noticed that the same comparison occurs in Philo.[5]

[1] Numenius, fr. 11 Leemans=Eus., *Praep. Ev.,* 11.21.

[2] *Les Sources de Plotin*, pp. 17 f.

[3] Numenius, test. 34 Leemans=Stob., I, p. 458.3 Wachsmuth; test. 33=
Stob., I, p. 365.5.

[4] Plot., I, vi, 7.4 ff. τὰ ἅγια τῶν ἱερῶν is not 'the Holy Celebrations of the
Mysteries' (MacKenna) but the inner shrines of temples, as appears from the
opening words of the next chapter and from VI, ix, 11.17, 'like one who has
penetrated to the interior of the sanctuary, leaving behind the statues in the
(outer) temple', which expresses the same thought in more Hellenic imagery.

[5] Both Cumont, who thought the reference was to Isiac cult (*Mon. Piot*, 25,
pp. 77 ff.), and Henry, who suggested (*Les États du texte de Plotin*, p. 211, n.) a

Speaking of the stripping away of bodily passions from the soul, Philo says 'That is why the High Priest will not enter the Holy of Holies in his sacred robe, but putting off the soul's tunic of opinion and imagery . . . will enter stripped of all colours and sounds'.[1] The thought is the same, though Plotinus avoids the specifically Jewish terms. But no one nowadays thinks that Plotinus had read Philo;[2] nor need we think so. The nature of Plotinus' immediate source is indicated by a passage from a Valentinian writer which Clement has preserved. There the entry of the Jewish High Priest into the Holy of Holies is said to symbolise the passage of the soul into the Intelligible World: as the priest takes off his ritual robe, so the soul makes itself naked; 'the human being', says the writer, 'becomes a carrier of God, being directly worked upon by the Lord and becoming as it were his body'.[3] This text goes beyond Philo: the High Priest's action is now definitely interpreted as a symbol of mystical experience, as it is in Plotinus. And it could be Plotinus' source: his essay *Against the Gnostics*, written after his

connection with the *Chaldaean Oracles* on the scanty evidence of Procl., *In Alc.*, 138.18 Cr., assumed that the comparison originated with Plotinus.

[1] Philo., *Leg. alleg.*, 2.56. Cf. Lev. xvi. 2–4.

[2] The unimpressive resemblances adduced by Guyot, *Les Réminiscences de Philon le Juif chez Plotin* (1906), are mostly to be explained by common sources in Plato and Poseidonius.

[3] Clem., *Exc. ex Theod.*, 27. Not all Clement's excerpts are Valentinian (some of them appear to express his own views), but I think this one is. The curious theory that the soul, after detaching itself from the earthly body, becomes 'as it were the body of the Power' (27.3), or 'the body of the Lord' (27.6), seems to correspond to the equally odd description of 'the material soul' as 'the body of the divine soul' in excerpt 51.2 which is generally recognised as Valentinian. If the speculation is merely Clement's personal fancy, it is hard to see how Plotinus came to know of it; he would scarcely consult the private notebooks of a Christian writer.

final breach with Gnosticism, seems to show considerable acquaintance with Valentinian teaching.[1] But we may also think of Numenius as a possible intermediary, since Numenius' special interest in things Jewish is well attested.[2]

What of mysticism within the Christian Church? As we have seen, there is much talk of assimilation to God, especially where Platonic influence is strong, and even, in certain authors, of 'divinisation' while still in the body. Clement likes to apply the traditional language of the Greek Mysteries to Christian religious experience: he often speaks, for example, of the 'vision' (*epopteia*) of God, though as a rule without making clear what he means by it.[3] The *Sentences* of Sextus tell us that 'in seeing God you will see yourself', and conversely that 'the soul of the wise man is God's mirror': for this way of talking there are two sources, in the *First Alcibiades* attributed to Plato, and in St Paul's second letter to the Corinthians.[4] But while there is the same general trend towards mysticism in the wide sense that we have observed in pagan

---

[1] Cf. Bouillet's notes to his translation, 1.491–544; H.-C. Puech in *Les Sources de Plotin*, pp. 162 f., 174, and (on Plotinus' relations with the Gnostics) pp. 183 f. The mystical strain in Valentinianism is evident in the recently published *Evangelium Veritatis*, e.g. where the writer says, 'It is by means of Unity that each one shall find himself. By means of Gnosis he shall purify himself of diversity with a view to Unity, by engulfing the Matter within himself like a flame, obscurity by light and death by life' (p. 25.10 ff. Malinine–Puech–Quispel).

[2] Cf. *Les Sources de Plotin*, pp. 5 f.

[3] At *Strom.* 7.11, Clement speaks of vision (ἐποπτεία) as 'the crowning advance open to the gnostic soul', but at 1.28 he equates it merely with theology or metaphysic. For other passages see *Pat. Lex.* s.v. ἐποπτεία.

[4] Sext., *Sent.*, 446 (cf. 577), 450. The sources are [Plat.], *Alc. i*, 133 C, where God is the mirror in which man sees his true self, and 2 Cor. iii. 18, where the sense is disputed (cf. Kirk, *Vision*, pp. 102–4).

authors, so far as my reading goes I have not found in any Christian writer of the period a single explicit reference to the possibility of *mystical union* in this life.

Origen has sometimes been claimed as an exception; but the most that Völker, the chief proponent of this view, is able to show is that Origen sometimes uses terms which *could* be applied to mystical union and were later so applied by others.[1] The sole passage in Origen which Völker claims to be a *description* of mystical union turns out to be little more than a paraphase of the words of St Paul which Origen is discussing.[2] More impressive is a passage in the *De principiis* where he pictures a state in which 'the mind will no longer be conscious of anything besides or other than God, but will think God and see God and hold God and God will be the mode and measure of its every movement'. But this is a picture of the final consummation, based on a verse in St John's Gospel; and it is accompanied by a warning that such bliss is not to be expected by an *embodied* soul even after death, much less before death.[3] It seems to be, as Father Daniélou says, 'a speculative theory . . . rather than a description of mystical experience'.[4] Recently, however, H. Crouzel[5] has asked whether it is likely that an author in whom so much of the language of later Christian mysticism appears was not himself in some degree a practising mystic. He calls attention to one of the few places where Origen speaks of

[1] W. Völker, *Das Vollkommenheitsideal des Origenes* (1931), pp. 117–44. See, *contra*, H.-C. Puech, *Rev. d'Hist. et Phil. Rel.* (1933).

[2] Völker, *op. cit.*, 124.

[3] Origen, *De princ.*, 3.6.1–3: cf. John xvii, 21.

[4] Daniélou, *Origen*, p. 297.

[5] H. Crouzel, *Origène et la connaissance mystique* (1961), p. 530.

his own experiences: in a sermon on the Song of Songs he says, 'Often, God is my witness, I have felt that the Bridegroom was approaching me and that he was, as far as may be, with me; then he suddenly vanished and I could not find what I was seeking'.[1] He adds that this expectation and disappointment has on some occasions recurred several times. On this evidence Origen should perhaps be classed as a mystic *manqué*. Certainly he possessed the concept of mystical union, and set a high value on it; he thus prepared the way for Gregory of Nyssa, whom he strongly influenced and who is usually called the first Christian mystic.

I cannot here say much about the mysticism of Gregory, who in any case falls outside the limits of our period. But I should like to raise the question of his debt to Plotinus. This has never been fully examined, but similarities of diction as well as thought seem to me to make it fairly certain that he had read at least one or two of Plotinus' more popular esssays. He holds, for example, as Plotinus did, that the soul is *naturally* united to God, and like him compares its fallen state to that of a man covered with mud, which must be washed off before he can return to his natural condition. But where Plotinus says that 'his task is to be what he once was', Gregory makes a silent correction: he insists that the return is 'not our task' but God's.[2] This insistence on the intervention of grace seems

---

[1] Origen, *Hom. in Cant.*, 1.7 (*G.C.S.* vɪɪɪ, 39.16). It may be significant that Origen was apparently the first to identify the 'Bride' in the Song of Songs with the individual soul; previous Christian commentators had identified her with the Church.

[2] Greg. Nyss., *P.G.* 46, 372 ʙᴄ.: cf. Plot., ɪ, vi, 5.43 ff. Apparent echoes of this popular essay ($\pi\epsilon\rho i$ $\tau o\hat{v}$ $\kappa a\lambda o\hat{v}$) are especially frequent in Gregory, e.g. Greg., *P.G.* 44, 541 ᴅ ff. is very close in language as well as thought to

to be the main feature which distinguishes Gregory's mysticism from that of Plotinus. In their account of mystical union the two writers agree closely, and I find it hard to accept Daniélou's claim that this agreement in language 'conceals wholly different realities'.[1] Like Plotinus, Gregory describes it as an awakening from the body, or an ascent to a place of watch; as in Plotinus, it is less a vision than an awareness of the divine presence; as in Plotinus, the soul becomes simple and unified, and takes on the quality of light, being identical with what it apprehends.[2] I think Gregory had enjoyed the same experience as Plotinus; but I think he also knew what Plotinus had said about it, and took over his descriptive vocabulary. To that extent and in that sense Christian mysticism springs from a pagan source.[3]

Plot., I, vi, 9.8 ff.; cf. also 46, 364 C with 1.20; 44, 428 C and 1145 AB with 8.16 ff.; 46, 173 D with 9.29 ff. The same essay was exploited by Basil (Henry, *États du texte de Plotin* (1938), p. 175), by Ambrose, whether at first hand or through a Greek intermediary (Courcelle, *Rev. de Phil.*, 76 (1950), pp. 29 ff.; Theiler, *Gnomon*, 25 (1953), pp. 113 ff.), and also by Augustine.

[1] J. Daniélou, *Platonisme et théologie mystique*, p. 233. His contention that Gregory's thought, as distinct from his language, is 'purely Christian' (*ibid.*, p. 9) may be contrasted with the opinion of Cherniss that 'but for some few orthodox dogmas which he could not circumvent, Gregory has merely applied Christian names to Plato's doctrine and called it Christian theology' (*The Platonism of Gregory of Nyssa* (1930), p. 62). Both judgements are surely a little extreme.

[2] Awakening from the body, Plot., IV, viii, 1.1; Greg. 44, 996 A-D. σκοπιά, Plot., IV, iv, 5.10; Greg., 44, 453 A (cf. also Numenius, fr. 11, quoted above, p. 93 and Plato, *Rep.*, 445 C). Divine presence, Plot., VI, ix, 8.33, etc.; Greg., 44, 1001 BC. ἅπλωσις, Plot., VI, ix, 11.23; Greg., 46, 93 C. Soul becoming φῶς, Plot., I, vi, 9.18 ff.; Greg. 44, 869 A. Cf. also Plot., III, viii, 10.5 ff. with Greg. 44, 1000 AB (God compared to an inexhaustible fountain); Plot., VI, ix, 8.38 with Greg. 44, 508 B (souls as a choir looking to God as their coryphaeus). I suspect that a fuller study by some one who knows both authors thoroughly would yield many further parallels.

[3] On the secondary place of mysticism in the early Christian tradition, and its derivative character, see A.-J. Festugière, *L'Enfant d'Agrigente* (1950), pp. 127–48.

To sum up. Within our period only Plotinus and Porphyry are known to have practised mysticism in the
strictest sense. But mystical experience admits of degrees,
and Plotinian mysticism is not an isolated phenomenon.
The tendency towards introvertive mystical *theory* is
strongly marked in the philosophy of the second century,
and in Numenius at least it is expressed in a manner suggestive of actual experience. We saw also that something
resembling extrovertive mysticism appeared in a Gnostic
and in a Hermetic text. And if we accept as 'mystical' in
the wide sense *any* attempt to build a psychological
bridge between man and Deity, then mysticism may be
said to be endemic in nearly all the religious thought of
the period, growing in strength from Marcus Aurelius to
Plotinus and from Justin to Origen. Nor need that surprise
us. As Festugière has rightly said, 'misery and mysticism
are related facts'.[1] From a world so impoverished intel-
lectually, so insecure materially, so filled with fear and
hatred as the world of the third century, any path that
promised escape must have attracted serious minds.
Many besides Plotinus must have given a new meaning to
the words of Agamemnon in Homer, 'Let us flee to our

[1] A.-J. Festugière, 'Cadre de la mystique hellénistique', in *Mélanges Goguel*
(1950), p. 84. The remark of Lucretius, 'multoque in rebus acerbis acrius
advertunt animos ad religionem' (3.53), seems to apply no less to mysticism
than to the external cult which Lucretius had in mind. W. Nestle, *N. Jahrbb.*,
1922, pp. 137–57, while recognising that there are no 'mystical periods' in the
history of classical Greece, noted four periods of political and social distur-
bance which gave rise to movements that can be called in the wide sense
'mystical', namely the sixth century B.C. (Pythagoras, Orphism); the after-
math of the Peloponnesian War (Plato); the first century B.C. (Poseidonius,
Neopythagoreanism); and the third century A.D. (Plotinus). I do not suggest
that explanations of this type are exhaustive (see p. 4, n. 2), but they are
surely relevant up to a point.

own country.'[1] That advice might stand as a motto for the whole period. The entire culture, pagan as well as Christian, was moving into a phase in which religion was to be coextensive with life, and the quest for God was to cast its shadow over all other human activities.

[1] Plot. I, vi, 8.16, echoed by Gregory, 44, 1145 B, and by Augustine, *Civ. Dei*, 9.17. The phrase comes from the *Iliad* (2.140), but Plotinus has the *Odyssey* in mind: he goes on to speak of Odysseus' flight from Circe and Calypso as a type of the soul's escape from sensuous beauty. The passage has a significant graphic counterpart in one of the Christian-Gnostic frescoes which decorate a third-century tomb near the Viale Manzoni in Rome: it appears to depict the return of Odysseus as a type of the soul's return 'to its own country' (J. Carcopino, *De Pythagore aux Apôtres*, pp. 175–211). Both Plotinus and the Gnostic painter are probably drawing on a Pythagorean source (Carcopino, *loc. cit.*; F. Buffière, *Les Mythes d'Homère et la pensée grecque*, pp. 413–18; M. Detienne, *Homère, Hésiode et Pythagore*, pp. 52–60); Numenius had allegorised the *Odyssey* in a similar manner (test. 45 Leemans, *apud* Porph. *Ant. nymph.* 34).

CHAPTER IV

THE DIALOGUE OF PAGANISM
WITH CHRISTIANITY

Uno itinere non potest perveniri ad tam grande secretum.
SYMMACHUS

U P to now I have been dealing with attitudes and experiences which were for the most part common to pagans and Christians—at any rate to some pagans and some Christians. But I must not leave the impression that in my opinion there were no important differences between paganism and Christianity in our period. In this final chapter I shall say something about pagan views of Christianity and Christian views of paganism as they emerge in the literature of the time. It is a large and complicated subject: to treat it fully a whole course of lectures would be needed.[1] So I shall have to

[1] The standard work on the pagan side of the dialogue is Labriolle's *Réaction*, a brilliant book whose only fault is that the author's strong Christian convictions occasionally make him a little unfair to the pagan writers. The opposite bias is evident in W. Nestle's essay, 'Die Haupteinwände des antiken Denkens gegen das Christentum', *Arch. f. Rel.*, 37 (1941–2), pp. 51–100. Celsus' *True Account* is known only from the extensive quotations in Origen's *Contra Celsum* (ed. Koetschau, *G.C.S.*; English translation by H. Chadwick (1953), with valuable introduction and brief notes). For an attempt to reconstruct it see R. Bader, *Der Ἀληθὴς Λόγος des Celsus* (1940); for discussion, L. Rougier, *Celse* (1925), A. Miura-Stange, *Celsus u. Origenes* (1926), and C. Andresen, *Logos und Nomos* (1955). The fragments of Porphyry's *Adversus Christianos* were collected by Harnack, *Abh. Akad. Berl., Phil.-Hist. Kl.*, 1916, Nr. 1; cf. J. Bidez, *Vie de Porphyre* (1913), pp. 65–79; J. Geffcken, *Der Ausgang des gr.-röm. Heidentums* (1920), pp. 56–77; A. B. Hulen, *Porphyry's Work Against the Christians* (1933).

limit myself to a few dominant themes; and in choosing these I shall have less regard to doctrinal disputes than to those differences of feeling which seem to constitute a psychological dividing line.

We should begin by getting two points clear. In the first place, the debate was conducted at many different intellectual and social levels. It engaged the energies of cultivated scholars like Origen and Porphyry; but it must also have been fought out, frequently and bitterly, in the council-chambers of Greek cities, in the market-places of North African villages, and in thousands of humble homes. Our knowledge of the dialogue at these levels is, alas, very limited, but what we do know or guess concerning it should be kept separate from the more sophisticated dialogue of the learned. Secondly, the debate was not a static one. Both Christianity and pagan philosophy were in continuous process of change and development throughout the period, and the relationship between them changed accordingly. We can distinguish three phases in the growth of their relationship.

At the beginning of the period neither pagan nor Christian thought formed a closed or unified system. Greek philosophy was groping towards the synthesis which Plotinus was to achieve a century later, but there was as yet little agreement, even among the adherents of the now increasingly fashionable Platonism. As for the Christians, according to Celsus they were split into many warring sects, which had little or nothing in common save the name of Christian.[1] This is surely an exaggeration; but it is certain that there was as yet no authoritative

---

[1] *Apud* Origen, *c. Cels.*, 3.10–12.

Christian creed nor any fixed canon of Christian scripture. The Muratorian fragment, commonly dated about 180, excludes the Epistle to the Hebrews and includes the Apocalypse of Peter; some Roman churchmen still rejected St John's Gospel, and many rejected the Apocalypse of John; Hermas, on the other hand, was thought even by Origen to be divinely inspired, and a great variety of apocryphal Gospels, Acts and Apocalypses circulated among the faithful.[1] Even the text of the Evangelists could still be tampered with: Marcion had rewritten Luke, and Clement of Alexandria knows of a 'secret' version of Mark which he considers basically genuine though interpolated by Gnostics for their own wicked purposes.[2] Orthodoxy was not yet clearly marked off from heresy: it was easy to slide from one to the other, as Tatian passed from orthodoxy to Valentinianism, and Tertullian to Montanism. If Celsus sometimes confused Christianity with Gnosticism, as Origen alleges,[3] it is probable that his confusion was shared by a good many contemporary Christians.

It is at this point that the dialogue with paganism be-

[1] Rejection of St John, Epiphanius, *Haer.*, 51.3; acceptance of Hermas, Iren., *Haer.*, 4.20.2; Origen, *Princ.*, 4.2.4. Cf. Eus., *Hist. Eccl.*, 3.25, and Harnack's discussion in his *Origin of the New Testament* (Eng. trans., 1925). It is significant that by the end of our period St John seems to be the most highly esteemed of the Evangelists. His Logos-doctrine appealed to the philosophers: Amelius, the pupil of Plotinus, cited it with approval (*apud* Eus., *Praep. Ev.*, 11.19.1); and a Platonist quoted by Augustine thought that the opening words of St John's Gospel 'should be written in letters of gold and set up to be read in the highest places of all churches' (*Civ. Dei*, 10.29).

[2] This is stated in a recently discovered letter of Clement: see W. Jaeger, *Early Christianity and Greek Paideia* (1962), pp. 56 f. and 132. Cf. Celsus' claim that some Christians 'alter the original text of the gospel three or four or several times over, and change its character to enable them to deny difficulties in face of criticism' (*c. Cels.*, 2.27).

[3] *C. Cels.*, 5.61 f.; 6.24 ff.

gins. The 'Apostolic Fathers' had written only for their fellow-Christians. Now the 'Apologists' emerge from their ideological ghetto and for the first time state the case for Christianity to the world of educated pagans— not so much in the expectation of converting them as in the hope of persuading them to call off the intermittent local persecutions from which the Church at this period suffered. And it was also in the latter part of the second century that a pagan intellectual for the first time took Christianity seriously. What to Pliny the Younger had been only a tiresome administrative nuisance, what to Lucian and even to Galen was no more than a psychological curiosity, appeared to Celsus as an actual menace to the stability and security of the Empire: with remarkable prescience he saw the Church as a potential State within the State, whose continued growth threatened in his opinion to disrupt the bonds of society and would end by letting in the barbarians.[1] He expressed his views in a book called *The True Teaching*, which aimed both at checking the spread of Christianity and at persuading Christians to be better citizens. It is thought to have been published under Marcus Aurelius, perhaps about the year 178.[2] If that date is right, it held the field, apparently unanswered, for two generations.

The second phase extends from 203, the year in which

---

[1] *C. Cels.*, 3.55; 8.35; and especially 8.68–75. Cf. H. Chadwick's introduction, pp. xxi f.

[2] On Celsus' date see H. Chadwick, introduction, pp. xxvi ff. But the evidence is very slender. It is probable that Celsus had read Justin and designed his book as a reply to Justin, though he does not name him (Andresen, pp. 345–72; A. D. Nock, *J.T.S.*, N.S. 7 (1956), pp. 316 f.). Celsus' title seems to mean 'the true (i.e. traditional) theological doctrine': see A. Wifstrand, 'Die Wahre Lehre des Kelsos', *Kong. Hum. Vetenskapsfundet i Lund, Aarsberättelse* 1941–2.

the youthful Origen began to teach at Alexandria, to 248 or thereabouts, when as an elderly man he published his *Contra Celsum*. For the people of the Empire it was a time of increasing insecurity and misery; for the Church it was a time of relative freedom from persecution, of steady numerical growth, and above all of swift intellectual advance. Clement of Alexandria had perceived that if Christianity was to be more than a religion for the uneducated it must come to terms with Greek philosophy and Greek science; simple-minded Christians must no longer 'fear philosophy as children fear a scarecrow';[1] Tertullian's maxim, 'nobis curiositate opus non est post Christum Iesum',[2] was seen to be a fatal bar to the conversion of the intelligent. Origen put himself to school with the pagan philosopher Ammonius Saccas, who was at a later date Plotinus' teacher. His own pupils were instructed not only in philosophy but in mathematics and natural science; his educational plan was based on Plato's, and did not differ in essentials from that of Plotinus.[3] Henceforth the dialogue with paganism was to be a dialogue between intellectual equals; indeed in the *Contra Celsum* Origen adopts, with some justification, a tone of intellectual superiority.[4] With the extensive

[1] Clem., *Strom.*, 6.80; cf. 6.93.

[2] Tert., *De praescript. haer.*, p. 9.18 Kroymann. Cf. also *De anima*, 1 f.

[3] Eus., *Hist. Eccl.*, 6.18.3 f.; Greg. Thaum., *Paneg. in Origenem*, 15. Cf. Porph., *Vit. Plot.*, 14.

[4] Cf. e.g. *c. Cels.*, 2.32, where Origen accuses Celsus of muffing his chances: he has missed the discrepancy between the genealogies of Jesus, 'which is a problem discussed even among Christians, and which some bring forward as a charge against them'. 'Origen feels that he could have made a far more effective case against Christianity than Celsus did' (Miura-Stange, *Celsus und Origenes*, p. 137, n. 1). On his use of pagan philosophical arguments against Celsus see H. Chadwick, *J.T.S.*, 48 (1947), pp. 34–49.

concessions which he made to Platonism I shall deal later.

On the pagan side there are signs at this time of a desire to absorb Christ into the Establishment, as so many earlier gods had been absorbed, or at any rate to state the terms on which peaceful coexistence could be considered. It may well have been with some such purpose in mind that Julia Mamaea, the Empress Mother, invited Origen to her court; we are told that her son, the Emperor Alexander Severus, kept in his private chapel statues of Abraham, Orpheus, Christ and Apollonius of Tyana, four mighty *prophetai* to all of whom he paid the same reverence.[1] He was not alone in adopting this attitude: about the same date the Gnostic Carpocrates was preaching a similar comprehensive cult—if we can believe Irenaeus and Augustine, his followers worshipped images of Homer, Pythagoras, Plato, Aristotle, Christ and St Paul.[2] The same spirit is illustrated in the undated letter of a Syrian named Serapion in which he cites Christ, 'the wise king of the Jews', along with Socrates and Pythagoras, as an example of a sage whose teaching has survived unjust persecution.[3] To the same period probably belong the two oracles of Hecate quoted by Porphyry in his early work *On the Philosophy of Oracles*. In answer to the ques-

---

[1] Eus., *Hist. Eccl.*, 6.21.3; Lampridius, *Alex.*, 29. The Severan dynasty (A.D. 193–235) had a strong leaning, not towards Christianity in particular, but towards oriental cults in general: cf. A. D. Nock, *Conversion*, pp. 128 f.

[2] Iren., *Haer.*, 1.25.6; Aug., *Haer.*, 7 (*P.L.* 42, p. 27). Gnosticism was equally hospitable to the supposed teaching of oriental sages: the Gnostic Prodicus possessed 'secret books' of Zoroaster (Clem., *Strom.*, 1.69.6, cf. Porph., *Vit. Plot.*, 16); revelations in the names of Zostrianus and Hermes Trismegistos were included in the Gnostic library at Nag-Hammadi; Mani reckoned Buddha and Zoroaster, as well as Jesus, among his divinely-sent forerunners (C. Schmidt, *Sitzb. Berl.*, 1933, pp. 56 f.).

[3] *P. Lond.* 987.

tion whether Christ were a god, Hecate replied, in substance, that Christ was a man of outstanding piety but
that in mistaking him for a god his followers had fallen
into grave error. From which Porphyry concluded that
'we should not speak ill of Christ but should pity the folly
of mankind'.[1]

The temper of the third phase is very different. It begins
with the Decian persecution in 249, the first systematic
attempt to exterminate Christianity by depriving the
Church of its leaders, and one which might perhaps have
succeeded if it had not been cut short by Decius' death in
battle.[2] It ends with the Great Persecution under Diocletian and Galerius, which produced innumerable rene-
gades but failed to shake the hard core of believers,
though for ten years they were treated as outlaws. In the
interval, helped by the appalling social and economic
conditions of the years 250 to 284, the Church had gained
rapidly in numbers and influence. It was in this interval,
probably about 270, that Porphyry produced his bitter
book *Against the Christians*, which found many imitators

[1] Eus., *Dem. Ev.*, 3.7; Aug., *Civ. Dei*, 19.23.2 ff. (=Wolff, *Porphyrii de phil.
ex orac. reliquiae*, 180 ff.). Cf. Amelius' favourable reference to St John's
Gospel (p. 104, n. 1).
[2] Cf. A. Alföldi, *C.A.H.*, XII, pp. 202 f.; F. C. Burkitt, *ibid.*, p. 521; and
W. H. C. Frend in *Past and Present*, 16 (1959), pp. 14–16. The worst ancient
persecutions were of course incomparably less severe than Hitler's massacre of
the Jews. The Christian clergy, and the most prominent of the laity, were vic-
timised; but save in exceptional circumstances 'the ordinary Christian who did
not insist on openly parading his confession of faith was most unlikely to become a victim of the persecution at all' (G. de Ste Croix, *Harv. Theol. Rev.*, 47
(1954), p. 104). As to the motives behind these persecutions we have little
evidence. According to some historians they were mainly or even exclusively
political; according to others, mainly religious. But the question is hardly to be
answered in terms of a simple 'either–or': Hitler's case should have taught us
how inextricably religious or racial fanaticism can be intertwined with purely
practical motives such as the search for scapegoats.

in the following years but also provoked many replies from the Christian side. In it he expressed the alarm which was now felt by all religious-minded pagans. He speaks of Christianity as a doctrine which is preached in the remotest corners of the world; he notes how at Rome the cult of Jesus is replacing that of Asclepius; and he notes also a new sign of Christian confidence and Christian wealth—they are building themselves large churches everywhere.[1] He does not call for persecution; indeed, he seems to have spoken with pity of the many Christians whom the teaching of their Church has caused 'to be inhumanely punished'.[2] His successors were less scrupulous. Hierocles, author of a treatise entitled *The Lovers of Truth*, in which he exalted Apollonius of Tyana as a rival to Christ, was also one of the instigators of the Great Persecution, and as a Provincial Governor was active in carrying it out.[3] He illustrates not only the alliance of the pagan intellectuals with the Establishment but also the transformation of Neoplatonism into a religion with its own saints and miracle-workers. Both were defensive reactions against the advance of Christianity; both were to be exemplified on a larger scale during the brief reign of the Emperor Julian.

---

[1] Porph., *Adv. Christ.*, frs. 13; 80; 76.27. Cf. Eus., *Hist. Eccl.*, 8.1.5, and Harnack, *Mission*, II, pp. 85–8. The inscriptional evidence suggests a steep decline in pagan cult in the second half of the third century: see Geffcken, *Ausgang*, 20–5, and Frend in *Past and Present*, 16 (1959), pp. 20–2.

[2] *Adv. Christ.*, fr. 36.9: cf. J. Bidez, *Vie de Porphyre* (1913), p. 68, n. 1. Against this Labriolle (*Réaction*, p. 286, n. 1) adduced a reference to 'just punishments' at fr. 1.14; but we have no means of telling how much of the language of this so-called fragment (at best a paraphrase) goes back to Porphyry.

[3] The evidence about Hierocles is collected by Labriolle, *Réaction*, pp. 306–10. He is not to be confused with the later Neoplatonist who wrote an extant commentary on the *Golden Verses*.

These changing relationships were naturally accompanied by some change in the character of the arguments used, though old arguments were often repeated after they had lost their force. For the dialogue at the popular level 'argument' is hardly the right word: it consisted mainly of invective. All our authorities, from Tacitus to Origen, testify to the bitter feelings of hostility which Christianity aroused in the pagan masses. The Christians, says Tacitus, were 'hated for their vices'; they were considered enemies of the human race: that was why the story of their responsibility for the Great Fire was so readily accepted.[1] 'The people of Christ', says Origen with a touch of pride, 'are hated by all nations, even by those who dwell in the remotest parts of the world.'[2] At Lyons in 177 the entire Christian community would have been dragged from their houses and beaten to death by the mob if the authorities had not intervened and substituted legal torture for lynching. It seems likely that many of the local persecutions in the second century were forced on reluctant Provincial Governors by popular feeling. Pliny the Younger was faced with anonymous denunciations containing long lists of names (which Trajan very properly advised him to disregard); at Lyons pagan slaves denounced their Christian masters; and even the systematic persecution under Decius was preceded by mob violence at Alexandria.

[1] Tac., *Ann.*, 15.44.3, 'per flagitia invisos . . . 5 haud proinde in crimine incendii quam odio humani generis convicti sunt'. Cf. Tert., *Apol.*, 37, 'hostes maluistis vocare generis humani Christianos'.
[2] *Comm. ser.* 39 *in Mt.* (vol. iv, p. 269 Lommatzsch). Such hostility was not, however, universal: at Alexandria during the Great Persecution many pagans concealed fugitive Christians from the police.

Why were the Christians so unpopular? The evidence points to a number of reasons, in addition to the generalised need for some one to kick which has always been an unacknowledged but influential element of human nature. Initially, no doubt, they shared the long-established unpopularity of the Jews: it seems that their first appearance in pagan records was as a dissident Jewish sect who at the instigation of one 'Chrestos' had engaged in faction-fights with their fellow Jews in the streets of Rome.[1] Like the Jews, they appeared to be 'godless' people who paid no proper respect to images and temples. But whereas the Jews were an ancient nation, and as such legally entitled to follow their ancestral custom in matters of religion, the Christians as an upstart sect of mixed nationality could claim no such privilege. They appeared, moreover, to constitute a secret society, whose members recognised each other by private signs, as gypsies do today, and were bound together by some mysterious intimacy.[2] 'They are a skulking breed', says the pagan in Minucius; 'they shun the light of day.'[3] What did they do behind their closed doors when the unbaptised were excluded? The old dark suspicions that had always been felt about secret associations were easily aroused against the Christians: it was said that like the Dionysiac societies suppressed in

[1] Suet., *Claud.*, 25.3. The confusion displayed in the words 'impulsore Chresto' suggests a contemporary police record: a later source would surely have been better informed. Cf. H. Jaune, 'Impulsore Chresto', *Mél. Bidez* (1934), pp. 531–53.

[2] Origen, *c. Cels.*, 1.1; Min. Felix, 9, 'occultis se notis et insignibus noscunt et amant mutuo paene antequam noverint . . . se promisce appellant fratres et sorores'. Cf. the secret signs used by Dionysiac initiates (Plaut., *Miles*, 1016; Apul., *Apol.*, 56).

[3] Min. Felix, 8, 'latebrosa et lucifugax natio'. Pythagoreans were disliked on similar grounds: Seneca calls them 'invidiosa turbae schola', *N.Q.*, 7.32.2.

186 B.C. they indulged in incestuous orgies, and like the Catilinarians practised ritual baby-eating.[1] These were presumably the 'vices' (*flagitia*) that Tacitus had in mind. Pliny thought it his duty to investigate these charges, but had to report that even with the help of torture he could find no evidence for them. Nevertheless they were quoted as fact by Fronto, the tutor of Marcus Aurelius, and we learn from Theophilus of Antioch that they were still widely believed, even by the educated, as late as 180.[2] All the Apologists thought it necessary to refer to them, and Origen tells us that in his time they still deterred some people from having dealings with Christians;[3] Celsus and Porphyry, however, had the sense to ignore them.

To misinformation about Christian morals was added misunderstanding about Christian politics. Did not the sacred books of the sect predict the speedy end of the Ronma Empire and its replacement by the rule of the Christian God on earth? The Apologists might explain that the expected Kingdom was purely spiritual,[4] but

---

[1] On alleged 'orgies', Dionysiac and Christian, see M. Gelzer, *Hermes*, 71 (1936), pp. 285–6; on allegations of sacramental cannibalism see the detailed examination of texts by F. J. Dölger, *Ant. u. Chr.* IV (1934), pp. 188–228. Rumours that the Christians ate the flesh and drank the blood of a god may have helped to support the latter charge. But the Christians themselves did not hesitate to bring similar accusations against Carpocratians (Iren., *Haer.*, 1.20.2; Clem., *Strom.*, 3.10.1) and against Montanists (Epiphanius, *Haer.*, 48.14.5; Aug., *Haer.*, 26). Justin has heard such stories about various Gnostic sects but, to his credit, does not claim that they are true (*Apol. i*, 26.7). He considers that the slanders against the Christians were put about by evil spirits intent on discrediting Christianity (*ibid.*, 10.6).

[2] Min. Felix, 9 (cf. 31); Theophilus, *Ad Autol.*, 3.4. At the trial of the Lyons martyrs in 178 these charges were supported by the evidence of slaves, obtained under torture (Eus., *Hist. Eccl.*, 5.1.14).

[3] Origen, *c. Cels.*, 6.27.

[4] E.g. Justin, *Apol. i*, 11.1: 'Hearing that we expect a Kingdom, you rashly conclude that it must needs be a kingdom in the human sense.'

could they be believed? Christians did not behave like loyal citizens. To the average pagan their refusal to burn a few grains of incense on the Emperor's birthday must have appeared as a deliberate and insolent expression of disloyalty, rather like refusing to stand up when the national anthem is played. The Apologists tried to explain that they meant no disrespect to the national symbol: they were quite happy to pray for the Emperor, and to acknowledge him as a being second only to God.[1] But this was not good enough either for the masses or for the law. To the modern student it may seem that this was a matter on which with a little good will a sensible compromise could have been reached. But on this issue the Christians displayed that 'invincible obstinacy' which struck Pliny as their most offensive characteristic. No doubt their spokesmen felt that even the most formal concession to pagan cult would lead in the end to Christianity being swallowed up and digested in the all-embracing maw of Graeco-Roman paganism as the other oriental religions had been.[2] Hence the charge of 'walling themselves off from the rest of mankind' which Celsus brings against them.[3] Celsus further complains that at a time when the Empire is in grave danger from the barbarians Christians shirk their duty as citizens by refusing to serve in the army or even in civilian offices. Origen's reply, that Christians by their prayers do more to help the Empire 'than those

[1] Tert., *Apol.*, 30; 39. Cf. Harnack, *Mission*, I, pp. 295–8; A. D. Nock, *Conversion*, pp. 227–9; N. H. Baynes in *C.A.H.*, XII, pp. 657–9.

[2] Cf. A. D. Nock, *Harv. Theol. Rev.*, 25 (1932), pp. 354 f. The Gnostics were in general more accommodating, and appear to have enjoyed in consequence a relative immunity from persecution: see W. H. C. Frend, 'The Gnostic Sects and the Roman Empire', *J. Eccl. Hist.*, 5 (1954), pp. 25–37.

[3] Origen, *c. Cels.*, 8.2.

who appear to be doing the fighting', will hardly have impressed the man in the street; and his contention that Christians serve society by serving their Church was even less reassuring.[1] On this question, however, the Church's hand was forced by its own followers. Christians had their living to earn: Origen's pacifism was impracticable, still more so the rigorism of Tertullian, which would have excluded Christians from many employments, even that of teaching. There were already Christians in the army by the beginning of the third century if not earlier; by the end of it there were so many that Diocletian felt obliged to institute a purge.[2] By Porphyry's time the charge of lack of patriotism was out of date, and was apparently dropped.

More persistent—and harder to eradicate because less rational—was the notion that the Christians were responsible for every natural calamity: their 'atheism' had offended the gods. Tertullian gave witty expression to it in a well-known passage: 'If the Tiber floods the town or the Nile fails to flood the fields, if the sky stands still or the earth moves, if famine, if plague, the first reaction is "Christians to the lion!"'[3] Throughout the third century, when disasters were many and relief-measures inadequate or non-existent, the Christians served the hard-pressed administration as convenient scapegoats. In 235 a series

---

[1] Origen, *c. Cels.*, 8.68–75. Cf. Tert., *Apol.*, 38.3, 'nobis . . . nec ulla magis res aliena quam publica'. On the influence of the Church in diverting able men from the service of the State cf. Momigliano, *Conflict*, pp. 9 f.

[2] Cf. Harnack, *Mission*, II, pp. 52–64; N. H. Baynes in *C.A.H.*, XII, pp. 659 f.

[3] Tert., *Apol.*, 40. Earthquakes above all inspired religious terror: cf. Cic., *De harusp. resp.*, 20 ff., and the vivid first-hand description in Aelius Aristides, *Orat.*, 49.38.

of earthquakes in Asia Minor started a local persecution; in 248 even the man-made disaster of civil war was blamed by some on the Christians; about 270 Porphyry associated the frequent epidemics at Rome with the decline of the cult of Asclepius; and later Maximin Daia supported his persecution by the same sort of charges.[1] Sometimes the blame was put on Christian magic: if anything went wrong with the taking of the omens, a Christian had spoilt the ritual by secretly making the sign of the cross. Augustine quotes a popular saying, 'Thanks to the Christian the drought goes on'.[2]

One other ground of resentment, less often emphasised by recent writers but surely not less important, was the effect of Christianity on family life. Like all creeds which claim the *total* allegiance of the individual—like communism, for example, in our own day—early Christianity was a powerful divisive force. Every town and every house, says Eusebius, is divided by a civil war waged between Christians and idolaters. Justin tells of a Christian wife who was denounced by her pagan husband; Ter-

---

[1] Firmilian *apud* Cyprian, *Epist.* 75.10; Origen, *c. Cels.*, 3.15; Porph., *Adv. Christ.*, fr. 80; Maximinus *apud* Eus., *Hist. Eccl.*, 9.7.8 f. Arnobius tells us that the people behind these charges were the oracle-priests and diviners who saw their livelihood threatened by the advance of Christianity (*Adv. nat.*, 1.24); this seems likely in itself, and is supported by Lactantius' story about the *extispicium* (see next note). Melito applied the same principle on the positive side: writing under Marcus Aurelius, he claims that Christianity has brought the blessing of God on the Empire (*apud* Eus., *Hist. Eccl.*, 4.26.7 f.), whereas a pagan pamphleteer quoted by Lactantius (*Div. Inst.*, 5.2) promises that Diocletian's persecution will bring it. The real importance of this motive in stimulating persecution is rightly stressed by Geoffrey de Ste Croix, 'Why were the early Christians persecuted?', *Past and Present*, 26 (1963), 6 ff.—a valuable paper which was unfortunately not available until the present book was in the press.

[2] Lact., *Mort. pers.*, 10; Aug., *Civ. Dei*, 2.3.

tullian speaks of cases where wives have been repudiated or sons disinherited for turning Christian; in Perpetua's account of her relations with her father we see how a family could be torn asunder by religious differences.[1] For such situations the blame was naturally laid on the Christian missionaries. Celsus has an illuminating passage, too long to quote, about Christians who get hold of pagan children, encourage them to disobey their fathers and schoolmasters, and lure them into Christian conventicles; often they work on the womenfolk as well. Origen does not deny that this happens; and Jerome later paints an equally unfavourable picture of fanatical monks who worm themselves into the homes of the aristocracy and exploit the guilt-feelings of the women.[2] Christianity, like communism, was a domestic trouble-maker.

Yet in face of this formidable weight of prejudice Christianity survived and spread. Some of the forces which worked in its favour I shall mention later. But it will be convenient first to consider the dialogue on the learned level, where mutual vituperation was tempered with a modicum of rational argument.

What was the debate about? It touched on far more problems than I can mention here; but the main issues were not those which a modern Christian might expect. In the first place, it was not a debate between monotheism

[1] Eus., *Dem. Ev.*, 8.5; Justin, *Apol. ii*, 2; Tert., *Apol.*, 3; *Passio Perpetuae*, 3; 5; 6. Further examples were collected by Harnack, *Mission*, I, pp. 393–8.

[2] Origen, *c. Cels.*, 3.55; Jerome, *Epist.* 22.28; cf. Tatian, *Orat.*, 33.1. The unscrupulous methods of certain missionaries are already condemned in 2. Tim. iii 6, which Jerome quotes. But the Christians were not alone in giving this sort of offence: cf. Aelius Aristides, *Orat.*, 46 (II, p. 402 Dind.), where certain *soi-disants* 'philosophers' (Cynics?) are compared in this respect to 'the impious in Palestine'.

and polytheism. It has been said with some justification that Celsus was a stricter monotheist than Origen: certainly he judged the Christians blasphemous in setting another on the same level as the supreme God.[1] He himself retained, it is true, a kind of residual polytheism: he thought we should pay respect to the subordinate gods or daemons who are the servants and ministers of the supreme God. But Origen too believed that God employs 'invisible husbandmen and other Governors', and that these control 'not only the produce of the earth but also all flowing water and air', thus taking the place of the pagan vegetation gods.[2] He also, like nearly all Christians, believed in the reality and power of the pagan gods; he merely substituted a minus for a plus sign—they were not gods but demons or fallen angels.[3] Origen's world is peopled with a vast multitude of supernatural beings: each nation, like each individual, has both a good and a bad

---

[1] Origen, *c. Cels.*, 8.12, 14; cf. A. Miura-Stange, *Celsus u. Origenes*, pp. 113–19. At a later date Julian was to accuse the Christians of worshipping 'not one man only, but many poor wretches', with reference to the cult of martyrs (*Adv. Galil.*, 201 E, p. 198 Neumann).—Origen did not in fact put Christ on a level with the supreme God. His Christology was 'subordinationist' (*c. Cels.*, 7.57): he held that Christ was not good without qualification, but only by participation (*Princ.*, 1.2.13, fr. 6 Koetschau) like the δεύτερος θεός of Numenius (fr. 28 Leemans).

[2] Celsus' view, *c. Cels.*, 8.25; Origen's, 8.31. Cf. Max. Tyr., 17.5: two truths are universally accepted by Greeks and barbarians alike, that 'there is only one God, King and Father of all', and that 'there are many gods, children of God, who participate in his power'. For the daemons of the elements cf. Albinus, *Epitome*, 15.

[3] *C. Cels.*, 8.3–5. The same view (based on 1 Cor. x. 20) was taken by Justin and most of the Apologists, with the result that fear of evil spirits was an ever-present source of anxiety to Christian minds. An alternative theory, less harmful in its psychological effects, was that of Minucius Felix, who followed Euhemerus in regarding the pagan gods as merely deified men (*Oct.*, 22 f.). Cf. Nock, *Conversion*, pp. 221–6.

angel.¹ Porphyry's world has a similar mixed popula-
tion: the Christians, he says, call them angels; we call
them gods because they are near to the Godhead—but
why quarrel about a name? Like Celsus, he defends the
popular practice of offering sacrifice to these beings 'as a
token of good will and gratitude', but this forms no part
of his personal religion; for him the only true sacrifice is
the solitary communion of the soul with the supreme
God.² Nor is there any substantial difference between
pagan and Christian Platonists about the nature of this
supreme God: that God is incorporeal, passionless, un-
changing, and beyond the utmost reach of human
thought is common ground to Celsus and Origen; both
of them attack the anthropomorphic notions of the vul-
gar.³ Different peoples have called this God by different
names; but this too, according to the pagan thinkers, is a
quarrel about words.⁴ That such a God should take

¹ Origen, *Hom. in Luc.*, 13 (*G.C.S.* ix, 80); *c. Cels.*, 5.25–9. He equates his
'angels of the nations', who come from Deut. xxxii. 8 f., with Celsus' 'over-
seers', who come from Plato, *Polit.*, 271 D. For the two daemons of the individual, good and bad, we need not postulate an oriental source. This belief
was held by Plutarch (*Tranq. an.*, 15, 474 B), who quoted Empedocles (B 122)
in support; Lucilius appears to have named Eucleides of Megara as its origina-
tor (Censorinus, *De die natali*, 3.3). See P. Boyancé, *Rev. de Phil.*, ser. 3, 8
(1934), pp. 189–202.—Origen's angelology is still alive: for a detailed and
perfectly grave discussion of it see J. Daniélou, *Origen* (Eng. trans.), pp. 220–45.

² Gods equated with angels, and justification of sacrifice, *Adv. Christ.*, fr.
76; such cult does no harm, its neglect does no good, *Ad Marc.*, 18; Porphyry's
personal religion, *De abst.*, 2.34, 43, and *Ad Marc.*, 11.

³ *C. Cels.*, 6.61–5; 7.38; 7.45; 7.66. Celsus and Origen rely on the same
Platonic texts, especially *Rep.*, 509 B, *Epist.* ii, 312 E, and *Epist.* vii, 341 C. It
is no wonder that according to Augustine most of the Platonists of his day
have been converted to Christianity 'paucis mutatis verbis atque sententiis'
(*De vera religione*, 23). One is reminded of the remark attributed to Harnack,
that by the fourth century Christianity and paganism 'had two mythologies
but only one theology'.

⁴ *C. Cels.*, 1.24; 5.41. The same point was made by Maximus of Madaura,
Augustine's pagan friend: we call God by many names, since no man knows

human shape and suffer earthly humiliation is naturally incomprehensible to the pagans.[1] But both Origen and the Apologists try to meet this by treating Jesus less as an historical personality than as a Hellenistic 'second God', the timeless Logos which was God's agent in creating and governing the cosmos. The human qualities and human sufferings of Jesus play singularly little part in the propaganda of this period; they were felt as an embarrassment in the face of pagan criticism.[2]

Again, it would be a mistake to suppose that the debate was one between Christian rigorism and pagan laxity. The Christian and the Neoplatonic ethics of our period are not easily distinguishable. For both, as we have seen,[3]

---

the true one, but 'deus omnibus religionibus commune nomen est' (Aug., *Epist.* 16.1). Origen falls back on the weak reply that the correctness of certain names is proved by their superior efficacy in spells and exorcisms (1.25; 5.45).

[1] 'No God or Son of God', says Celsus, 'has come down or could come down' (*c. Cels.*, 5.2). On the face of it, this may seem surprising: pagans were familiar both with 'dying gods' like Attis and Adonis and with epiphanies of Olympian deities. But the epiphanies were momentary, and the dying gods were chthonic from the outset; they were of the earth, they had not 'come down' in the Christian sense. The Dionysus of the *Bacchae* is at first sight a closer parallel (as Clement of Alexandria and the author of the *Christus Patiens* perceived), but the parallel holds good only on a docetist view: Dionysus 'comes down' to mock and to punish, not to suffer. Cf. A. D. Nock, *Gnomon*, 33 (1961), pp. 585–90.

[2] 'We are sometimes told that the unique attractiveness of the central figure of Christianity as presented in the Synoptic Gospels was a primary factor in the success of Christianity. I believe this idea to be a product of nineteenth-century idealism and humanitarianism. In early Christian literature those aspects of the Gospel picture which are now most prominent in homiletic writing are not stressed, and all the emphasis is on the superhuman qualities of Jesus, as foreshadowed by prophecy and shown by miracle and resurrection and teaching, and not on his winning humanity' (Nock, *Conversion*, p. 210). This is already true of the Pauline letters, where, as Bultmann says, 'Christ has lost his identity as an individual human figure' (*Primitive Christianity* (Eng. trans., 1956), p. 197).

[3] See above, p. 75.

the ideal aim is 'assimilation to God'; both are concerned with the salvation of the individual soul rather than with making the world a better place;[1] how many practical precepts they had in common we can see by comparing the Christian and the pagan versions of those *Sentences* of Sextus which I mentioned in chapter I. Celsus finds Christian ethics banal: they 'contain no teaching that is impressive or new'; the advice about turning the other cheek is old stuff, better expressed by Plato. And Origen for his part does not deny this: the difference, he says, is that the Christian preachers 'cook for the multitude', whereas Plato spices the same dish to please the gentry.[2] His admiration for Plato is hardly less than that of Celsus; but Plato is read only by the learned—Christianity, he seems at times to suggest, is Platonism for the many.

Had any cultivated pagan of the second century been asked to put in a few words the difference between his own view of life and the Christian one, he might reply that it was the difference between *logismos* and *pistis*, between reasoned conviction and blind faith. To any one brought up on classical Greek philosophy, *pistis* meant

[1] Porphyry, unlike Celsus, appears perfectly indifferent to social or politica considerations: 'the wise man', he says, 'needs only God' (*Ad Marc.*, 11). For the general Christian standpoint cf. Bultmann, *Primitive Christianity* (Eng. trans., p. 206): 'Primitive Christianity is quite uninterested in making the world a better place; it has no proposals for political or social reform.' But this did not, of course, exclude the exercise of practical φιλανθρωπία towards individuals (see below, pp. 136 f.).

[2] Celsus on Christian ethics, *c. Cels.*, 1.4; 7.58–9. Plato useless save to the highly educated, 6.1–2 (where Epictetus is said to be more valuable to the masses); 7.61. Cf. Julian's view of the Decalogue (*Adv. Christ.*, 152 D, pp. 188 f. Neumann): if we except the rules about monotheism and the Sabbath, the remaining commandments form part of the moral code of all peoples.

the lowest grade of cognition: it was the state of mind of the uneducated, who believe things on hearsay without being able to give reasons for their belief. St Paul, on the other hand, following Jewish tradition, had represented *pistis* as the very foundation of the Christian life. And what astonished all the early pagan observers, Lucian and Galen, Celsus and Marcus Aurelius, was the Christians' total reliance on unproved assertion—their willingness to die for the indemonstrable.[1] For Galen, a relatively sympathetic observer, the Christians possess three of the four cardinal virtues: they exhibit courage, self-control and justice; what they lack is *phronesis*, intellectual insight, the rational basis of the other three.[2] For Celsus they are the enemies of science: they are like quacks who warn people against the doctor, saying that knowledge is bad for the health of the soul.[3] Later on Porphyry seems to have repeated the same protest against 'an irrational and unexamined *pistis*'; and Julian exclaims, 'There is nothing in your philosophy beyond the one word "Believe!"'[4] But by Porphyry's time, and still more by Julian's, the situation had changed in two ways.

In the first place, Christians were now prepared, as we have noticed, to state a reasoned case. Athenagoras had

[1] Lucian, *Peregr.*, 13, Christian beliefs unsupported by evidence; Galen, *De puls. diff.*, 2.4 (VIII, 579 Kühn), Jews and Christians obey undemonstrated rules; Celsus *apud* Orig., *c. Cels.*, 1.9, 6.11, some Christians say, 'Ask no questions: just believe'; M. Ant., 11.3.2, Christians are ready to die, not on any reasoned ground but out of sheer contrariness (κατὰ ψιλὴν παράταξιν). Cf. Walzer's discussion in *Galen*, pp. 48–56.

[2] Galen in Walzer, *Galen*, p. 15 (the passage survives only in Arabic quotations); discussion, *ibid.*, pp. 65–74.

[3] *C. Cels.*, 3.75.

[4] Porph., *Adv. Christ.*, fr. 1.17 (cf. fr. 73); Julian *apud* Greg. Naz., *Orat.*, 4.102 (*P.G.* 35, p. 637).

already recognised the need for *logismos*;[1] Origen was ready to refute the pagans point by point, borrowing for the purpose all the weapons in the arsenal of Greek philosophy. His contempt for mere *pistis* is hardly less than that of Celsus. 'We accept it', he says, 'as useful for the multitude': it is the best that can be done for them, 'since, partly owing to the necessities of life and partly owing to human weakness, very few people are enthusiastic about rational thought'. And he goes on to point out, with justice, that pagans do not always choose their philosophy on purely rational grounds.[2]

In fact, while Origen and his successors were endeavouring to supplement authority by reason, pagan philosophy tended increasingly to replace reason by authority—and not only the authority of Plato, but the authority of Orphic poetry, of Hermetic theosophy, of obscure revelations like the *Chaldaean Oracles*. Plotinus resisted revelations of this type and set his pupils the task of exposing them;[3] but after Plotinus Neoplatonism became less a philosophy than a religion, whose followers were occupied like their Christian counterparts in expounding and reconciling sacred texts. For them too *pistis* became a basic requirement. Porphyry himself at the end of his life made *pistis* the first condition of the soul's approach to God, 'for we must believe (*pisteusai*) that in turning towards God is our only salvation'—without this faith,

[1] *Legat.*, 8, Athenagoras promises to produce τὸν λογισμὸν ἡμῶν τῆς πίστεως.

[2] *C. Cels.*, 1.9 f. The point about the accidental nature of men's choice of philosophies had already been made by Lucian, *Hermotimus*, 15 ff., and by Galen, *De ord. libr. suor.*, 1 (XIX, 50 K.): cf. Walzer, *Galen*, p. 19.

[3] Porph., *Vit. Plot.*, 16.

we cannot attain to truth, love or hope.[1] The same association of *pistis* with truth and love appears several times in Proclus.[2] Some have seen in it a conscious borrowing from Christianity, but I should myself prefer to regard it as an illustration of the old and true saying that 'we grow like what we hate'. If it were to fight Christianity on equal terms, Neoplatonism had to become a religion; and no religion can dispense with *pistis*—it was already demanded in the *Chaldaean Oracles* and in some of the *Hermetica*.[3]

The early Apologists had little to say about the per-

[1] Porph., *Ad Marc.*, 24.

[2] Procl., *In Alc.*, 51.15 Cr.: πίστις, ἀλήθεια and ἔρως are a triad of creative principles corresponding respectively to the Good, the Intelligible and the Beautiful. *In Tim.* 1.212.21 Diehl: to make the best use of prayer we need (among other things) πίστιν καὶ ἀλήθειαν καὶ ἔρωτα, ταύτην ἐκείνην τὴν τριάδα, καὶ ἐλπίδα τῶν ἀγαθῶν . . . ἵνα μόνος τις τῷ θεῷ μόνῳ συνῇ. *In Parm.*, 927.26 Cousin: πίστις, ἀλήθεια and ἔρως are τὰ σώζοντα τὰς ψυχὰς κατ' ἐπιτηδειότητα τὴν πρὸς ἐκεῖνα τρία συνάπτουσαν. Professor Armstrong has recently said that 'the *pistis* of Proclus is not Christian faith but Platonic firm rational confidence' (*Downside Rev.*, 1961, p. 116, n. 15). I do not myself think that it is either of these things: Proclus' immediate source must be (as Kroll saw, *De orac. Chald.*, p. 26) the *Chaldaean Oracles*, from which he quotes (*In Alc.*, 52.13) the line πάντα γὰρ ἐν τρισὶ τοῖσδε κυβερνᾶταί τε καὶ ἔστι. Cf. *Theol. Plat.*, 1.25, p. 62 Portus ἡ πρὸς αὐτὸ (sc. τὸ ἀγαθόν) συναφὴ καὶ ἕνωσις ὑπὸ τῶν θεολόγων πίστις ἀποκαλεῖται (where τῶν θεολόγων=Orac. Chald.). That Porphyry drew on the same source (as Theiler assumes, *Entretiens Hardt*, III, p. 87) is perhaps less certain: Porphyry's *pistis* is a state of mind, not a cosmological principle, and he names four qualities, not a triad as the *Oracles* did (though they admittedly mentioned ἐλπίς elsewhere). But this assumption is at any rate better founded than Harnack's view, that Porphyry borrowed from 1 Cor. xiii. 13 πίστις, ἐλπίς, ἀγάπη, or Reitzenstein's, that Porphyry and St Paul have a common source in some lost pre-Pauline pagan: on these speculations see P. Corssen, *Sokrates*, 7 (1919), pp. 18–30.

[3] For *pistis* in the *Hermetica* cf. *Corp. Herm.*, ix, 10, τὸ γὰρ νοῆσαί ἐστι τὸ πιστεῦσαι . . . καὶ περινοήσας τὰ πάντα . . . ἐπίστευσε, καὶ τῇ καλῇ πίστει ἐπανεπαύσατο, and the passages quoted by Festugière *ad loc*. Plotinus nowhere uses *pistis* in this sense (at VI, ix, 4.32 it has its ordinary Aristotelian meaning of '*prima facie* evidence').

sonality of Jesus or about the doctrine of atonement. Instead, they placed their main reliance on two arguments which their present-day successors have in general abandoned—the argument from miracles and the argument from prophecy. In this they were, of course, following the example of the New Testament writers. But miracles also played an important part in the propaganda of the various pagan cults.[1] The ancient debate on miracles was in the main a conflict not between believers and rationalists but between two sorts of believers. And what seems curious to a modern reader is that in our period neither party is prepared to assert positively that the miracles of the other party are fictitious. The earliest Apologist, Quadratus of Athens, argued that Jesus' miracles of healing were superior to the pagan ones, not because they were more genuine, but because they were more lasting:[2] it would appear that the early Christians, like good physicians, followed up their cases. Even Origen did not deny the occurrence of miracles at the shrine of Antinous in Egypt: he thought they were due to 'a demon established there', assisted by 'Egyptian magic and spells'.[3] More often he offers his reader alternative views: the healing miracles of Asclepius and the inspiration of the Pythia are probably *not* genuine, but if they are

---

[1] Especially those of Asclepius, Isis and Sarapis: cf. Nock, *Conversion*, pp. 83–98. On the Christian side, the insatiable appetite for miracles finds expression in the 'infancy gospels', the various apocryphal 'Acts' of apostles, and the martyrologies. Miracles are the favourite subjects of the oldest Christian art (Lietzmann, *Founding of the Church*, pp. 144–6).

[2] Eus., *Hist. Eccl.*, 4.3.2. Labriolle quotes a similar argument on the pagan side, based on the lasting efficacy of Apollonius' talismans (*Quaest. et Resp. ad orth.*, 34, ed. Harnack, *TU*, xxi, iv, p. 86).

[3] Origen, *c. Cels.*, 3.36. For these miracles cf. Dio Cassius, 69.11.

they are due to evil spirits.[1] Origen could not afford total scepticism about oracles; Eusebius could, since in his day damaging admissions had been obtained by torture from the official *prophetai*.[2] The pagan position is closely similar. For Celsus the New Testament miracles are 'monstrous tales', but if they were true they would be no proof of Jesus' divinity: like the operations of Egyptian magicians, they may be simply 'the practices of wicked men possessed by an evil *daemon*'.[3] Porphyry admits that the Christians 'have performed some wonders by their magic arts', but adds that 'to perform wonders is no great thing': Apollonius and Apuleius and countless others have done as much.[4] *Non est grande facere signa*: in a world where every one believed in magic,[5] miracles were both commonplace and morally suspect; they might serve to

---

[1] *C. Cels.*, 3.24–5; 7.3.

[2] Eus., *Praep. Ev.*, 4.2.10–12.

[3] *C. Cels.*, 1.68. Cf. 1.6, 'it was by magic that Jesus was able to do the miracles that he appeared to have done', and 1.38. Celsus puts these remarks into the mouth of a Jew, and according to Justin, *Dial.*, 69.7, this was in fact how the Jews explained the Gospel miracles. In polemical writing, as R. M. Grant observes, 'your magic is my miracle, and vice versa'.

[4] *Adv. Christ.*, fr. 4. Elsewhere, however, Porphyry seems to have put down certain Gospel miracles to false reporting: cf. fr. 49, the affair of the Gadarene swine probably fictitious, but if genuine then morally discreditable.

[5] Fear of magic was not confined to the ignorant. Men as highly educated as Plotinus and Libanius seriously believed themselves to have been the object of magical attack (cf. P. Merlan, *Isis*, 44 (1953), pp. 341–3; Campbell Bonner, *T.A.P.A.*, 63 (1932), pp. 34 ff.). And in Christian minds this fear was strongly reinforced by the fear of demons (pagan gods and planetary *archontes*). For them magic was not merely a compulsion exercised by human will on more or less neutral spirits; it enjoyed the active support and co-operation of evil powers. Hence the ruthlessly enforced laws of Constantius II and of Valentinian against magic: even protective or 'white' magic, which Constantine had expressly tolerated, was now made subject to the death penalty (cf. A. A. Barb in Momigliano, *Conflict*, pp. 100–25). Nevertheless magic continued to be practised; 'the main formal difference between Christian and pagan magic was one of nomenclature' (B. R. Rees, *J. Eg. Arch.*, 36 (1950), p. 88).

impress the masses, but arguments based on them were inevitably two-edged.

The argument from prophecy bulks large in Justin, and is urged repeatedly by Origen.[1] Celsus in reply pointed to the vagueness and generality of the Old Testament prophecies.[2] But his acquaintance with the Bible was limited, and Origen was able to convict him of missing important points.[3] Porphyry was a more formidable opponent. The best scholar of his time, he was accustomed to criticising documentary evidence, knew both Testaments thoroughly, and was equipped with a better knowledge of Hebrew than Origen had. Where Celsus was content with generalisations, not always well informed, Porphyry everywhere quotes biblical texts to justify his assertions. He takes a scholar's pleasure in convicting the Evangelists of false references to the Hebrew prophets, in pointing out contradictions between the different Gospel narratives, and in exposing the inconsistencies of St Paul.[4] He also has the scholar's typical weaknesses: some of his criticisms are pedantic, as when he

[1] Cf. Justin, *Apol. i*, 39–53; Origen, *c. Cels.*, 1.34–7, 49–57; 2.28–9; 3.2–4; 7.2–4, 16–20. Justin calls it 'the greatest and truest proof' of the truth of Christianity, *Apol. i*, 30.

[2] *C. Cels.*, 1.50; 2.28.

[3] *C. Cels.*, 1.34, 49; 2.37.

[4] False references, *Adv. Christ.*, frs. 9 and 10; contradictions, frs. 12, 15, 16; inconsistency of St Paul, frs. 30–3. Some Christian writers asserted that Porphyry was a renegade who had been beaten up by Christians in his youth and had left the Church out of personal pique (see Zeugnisse 20, 26 b and 29 in Harnack's edition). Harnack believed this, but it looks to me like a mere guess based on Porphyry's exceptional knowledge of Scripture and supported by a story which seeks to discredit his attack by ascribing it to a personal motive. Cf. Lactantius' similar suspicion that Hierocles was a renegade Christian (*Div. Inst.*, 5.2.12), and Porphyry's own mistaken guess that Origen was a renegade pagan (*Adv. Christ.*, fr. 39).

complains that the 'sea of Galilee' is not a sea but a lake, and therefore unlikely to experience storms; others are crudely unimaginative, as when he professes not to understand how the Kingdom of Heaven can be compared to a grain of mustard seed.[1] But at his best he is an impressive critic. He used Philo of Byblos to check the historical statements of the Old Testament, and he anticipated modern scholars in dating the Book of Daniel to the reign of Antiochus Epiphanes on sound historical grounds.[2] He was in fact the first man, so far as our knowledge goes, to apply the canons of historical criticism to the Bible.

On the Christian side the most impressive outcome of the dialogue is the grandiose attempt which Origen made in the *De principiis*[3] to produce a synthesis of Christianity and Platonism. I cannot here do justice to this remarkable book, but even a rapid survey will serve to show how far-reaching were his concessions to the pagan standpoint. He takes over the substance not only (as we have seen) of Plato's theology but also of the Platonic world-picture. The cosmos is a mighty living creature,

[1] *Adv. Christ.*, frs. 55, 54.
[2] *Adv. Christ.*, frs. 41, 43.
[3] Ed. Koetschau, *G.C.S.* vol. 5; Eng. trans., Butterworth, 1936. This early work of Origen is, unfortunately, preserved only in the Latin version by Rufinus, who admits that he has removed from it certain unorthodox views 'as interpolations'; but its original teaching can often if not always be recovered with the help of surviving quotations from the Greek. In later life Origen himself—perhaps under ecclesiastical pressure—abandoned or qualified some of the opinions expressed in it; and the problem is further complicated by subsequent confusion between Origen's personal views and those expressed by some of his more extreme followers. The teaching of the *De principiis* has been much discussed: see most recently C. Tresmontant, *Métaphysique du Christianisme* (1961), pp. 395–457, and F. Refoulé, *Rev. de l'hist. des rel.*, 163 (1963), pp. 11–52.

sustained and kept in being by the Logos, which functions like the Platonic world-soul.[1] Within it are many other living beings, including the stars which are themselves ensouled and may provide a future home for certain human souls.[2] The cosmos had indeed a beginning and will have an end, but it will be followed by a succession of other worlds:[3] the Resurrection is thus reduced to the status of an episode in cosmic history; the final *apocatastasis*, when all things will return to their original state, is infinitely remote.

Even more striking is the psychology of the *De principiis*, which is much closer to Plotinus than to St Paul. The soul is eternal not merely *a parte post* but also *a parte ante*, and not merely by divine grace but by its essential nature. It is indeed a created thing, but its creation, as in Plotinus, is outside of time.[4] Every soul was originally a pure intelligence, and every soul will eventually be restored to that condition.[5] But in the interval it must rise and fall many times: only on the assumption of past offences committed in past lives can the fact that we do not start level in the race for salvation be explained in a manner consistent with divine justice.[6] A human soul can rise to the status of an angel or sink to that of a devil; and Origen certainly toys with Plato's idea that it can be re-

[1] *Princ.*, 2.1.2. Cf. Porphyry's remark that 'about God and the world Origen thought like a Greek' (*Adv. Christ.*, fr. 39.29).

[2] *Princ.*, 1.7.2; 2.11.7; *c. Cels.*, 5.10–11. Stars as possible homes for human souls, *Hom. in Num.*, 28.2.

[3] *Princ.*, 2.3.4–5; 3.5.3.

[4] *Princ.*, 1.4.3–5. Cf. Plot., IV, iv, 15.16 ff.

[5] *Princ.*, 2.8.3.

[6] *Princ.*, 2.9.3–5. Cf. *c. Cels.*, 3.38, where he no longer commits himself to any theory but 'will refer the question to God'. For earthly life as requital of past offences cf. Plato, *Laws*, 872 E.

born in an animal body.[1] Between incarnations its fate depends on the life it has lived on earth. The bad will suffer purgation, but not eternally, since divine justice is always remedial, not vindictive. Hell is not an everlasting bonfire but a state of mind: it represents what Origen called 'the penalty and torture of the soul's want of cohesion'.[2] The good will dwell for a time in the Earthly Paradise; there God will organise a school for souls with angelic instructors, who will teach them the answers to all the questions that puzzled them on earth.[3] Origen provides a syllabus, on which the souls will eventually be examined; those who pass will be promoted to higher spheres and more advanced courses: Heaven is an endless university. In this state the souls will be furnished with bodies of subtler stuff than ours, but as they rise through the spheres these will be gradually sloughed off (as the pagan Platonists also held);[4] their final condition

---

[1] *Princ.*, 1.8.4 (as reported by Jerome and Gregory of Nyssa): cf. Courcelle's note in Momigliano, *Conflict*, pp. 186–8. Origen here goes further than many pagans in literal acceptance of Plato's teaching. Animal reincarnation, though accepted by Plotinus, was rejected by Porphyry (*apud* Aug., *Civ. Dei*, 10.30) and most of the later Neoplatonists, as also by the *Chaldaean Oracles* (p. 62 Kroll) and by the author of *Corp. Herm.* x, 19.

[2] Divine justice not vindictive, *Princ.*, 2.10.6; *Hom. in Ez.*, 12; and elsewhere. Punishment not eternal, *Princ.*, fr. 25; cf. *c. Cels.*, 5.16. Fires of Hell a metaphor for conscience, *Princ.*, 2.10.4–5 (cf. Lucr., 3.978 ff. and Philo, *Congr.*, 57).

[3] *Princ.*, 2.11.6. For the idea of progress after death cf. Clem., *Eclog.*, 57.5 (*G.C.S.* III, 154.8) and the myth in Plutarch's *De facie*; but no one else intellectualises it so severely as Origen. In Gregory of Nyssa it becomes a progress in mystical union (ἐπέκτασις), which will continue to all eternity (*P.G.* 44, 941 A).

[4] *Princ.*, 1.4.1 (as reported by Jerome) and fr. 19: cf. H. Koch, *Pronoia und Paideusis* (1932), p. 37; Daniélou, *Origen*, pp. 209–16. On the belief in 'subtler bodies', which was widespread from the second century onwards, see my edition of Proclus, *Elements of Theology*, appendix II.

will probably be bodiless—the 'spiritual body' of which St Paul spoke is only a temporary compromise.[1]

This bold rewriting of New Testament Christianity was rendered possible by an ingenious use of the time-honoured allegorical method. The art of twisting texts in this way, originally invented as a means of reading deep truths into Homer, had long been practised at Alexandria: the Jews had applied it to the Old Testament and the Gnostics to the New;[2] from them it was taken over first by Clement and then by Origen. To speculative minds it offered the only possible escape from the tyranny of the letter; despite its hopelessly unhistorical character it was thus in a sense an instrument of progress.[3] That 'the more reasonable among the Jews and Christians interpret these things allegorically' was already noted by Celsus. He protested against their abuse of the method, as did Por-

---

[1] *Princ.*, 3.6.1 (as reported by Jerome). This was an important concession to pagan opinion. No Christian doctrine was more shocking to educated men than the resurrection of the body. Celsus calls it 'revolting and impossible' (*c. Cels.*, 5.14); and Plotinus (who nowhere mentions the Christians by name) surely had it in mind when he wrote that 'the true awakening of the soul is a true resurrection ($\dot{\alpha}\nu\dot{\alpha}\sigma\tau\alpha\sigma\iota\varsigma$) not with the body but from the body' (III, vi, 6.71). Origen, though uneasy about it, will not reject it altogether (*Princ.*, 3.6. 4–9); but some second-century Christians did (Celsus, *loc. cit.*; 2 *Clem.*, 9.1; Justin, *Dial.*, 80.2), as Synesius did later. For the *simpliciores*, on the other hand, it was doubtless a major attraction. Human egotism will be satisfied with nothing less than the permanence of the ego, and of this the resurrection of the body appeared to give a firmer assurance than anything the Platonists could promise.

[2] Heracleon had produced an elaborate allegorical interpretation of the Gospel of St John in the interest of Valentinian theology; and Basileides had even succeeded in discovering the transmigration of souls in the Pauline epistles (fr. 3 Völker=Origen, *Comm. in Rom.*, 5.1). The Jewish food laws are already fantastically allegorised in the *Epistle of Barnabas*. Allegorical interpretation of the Old Testament was introduced to the pagan world by Numenius (frs. 19 and 32 Leemans=Origen, *c. Cels.*, 4.51), who perhaps drew on Philo.

[3] Cf. E. de Faye, *Clément d'Alexandrie* (1898), p. 210.

phyry later.[1] But here the critics were on weak ground: both Celsus and Porphyry had themselves used the same method to discover Platonism in Homer.[2] Christians and pagans were alike schoolmen: they could not challenge the authority of ancient texts; they could only evade it by reading back their own thoughts into them.[3]

When Origen wrote the *De principiis* Christian notions of eschatology were still in a state of flux, and for a long time they appear to have remained so.[4] Nearly two centuries later two Christian bishops, Synesius and Nemesius, could still profess belief in the pre-existence of the soul; the former could still doubt the resurrection of the body and the eventual destruction of the cosmos. And even the saintly Gregory of Nyssa, more than a century after Origen, could still reject eternal punishment, holding that all souls will at length be restored to their original paradisal state.[5] To an outside observer it may seem a major historical calamity that the last-named opinion failed to win acceptance by the Church. But biblical authority was too strong. After three centuries of con-

[1] Celsus *apud* Origen, *c. Cels.*, 4.48–51 (cf. 1.17); Porph., *Adv. Christ.*, fr. 39, Origen reads Greek philosophical doctrines into Jewish myths. Origen did in fact aim at 'demythologising' Judaism (*c. Cels.*, 5.42), pretty much as certain modern theologians wish to demythologise Christianity. By no other means could he make palatable to the educated what Gregory of Nyssa calls 'the hard, refractory bread of Scripture' (*Hom. in Cant.*, 7, P.G. 44, 925 B).

[2] *C. Cels.*, 6.42; Porph., *De antro nympharum*: cf. P. Courcelle, *Rev. Ét. Anc.* 46 (1944), pp. 65–93, and C. Andresen, *Logos und Nomos*, pp. 141–5. Origen is on similarly weak ground when he rejects the allegorical interpretation of pagan myths, *c. Cels.*, 3.23.

[3] Cf. my remarks in *J.R.S.*, 50 (1960), pp. 1 f. If the Freudians are right, this intellectual dependence is closely related to the guilt-feelings whose prevalence was noticed in ch. 1: they are two facets of the same character.

[4] Cf. Marrou in Momigliano, *Conflict*, pp. 145–9.

[5] Synesius, *Epist.* 105; Nemesius, *Nat. hom.*, 2, P.G. 40, 572 B; Greg. Nyss., P.G. 44, 1313 A; 46, 104 BC, 133 D.

troversy virtually all of Origen's innovations were condemned as heretical by an edict of Justinian in 543. It was not Origen but Augustine who determined the future pattern of Western Christianity. Nilsson laments that the Church threw out the baby with the bathwater, rejecting not only the superstitions of late paganism but 'the sound kernel of ancient science'.[1] One may question, however, whether the kernel could at this point have been saved at all. In the fourth century paganism appears as a kind of living corpse, which begins to collapse from the moment when the supporting hand of the State is withdrawn from it. And it is hard to believe that Julian's attempt to resuscitate it by a mixture of occultism and sermonising could have had any lasting success even if he had lived to enforce his programme. The vitality was gone: as Palladas expressed it, speaking for the last generations of educated pagans, 'If we are alive, then life itself is dead[2].' One reason for the success of Christianity was simply the weakness and weariness of the opposition: paganism had lost faith both in science and in itself.

Christianity, on the other hand, was judged to be worth living for because it was seen to be worth dying for. It is evident that Lucian, Marcus Aurelius, Galen and Celsus were all, despite themselves, impressed by the courage of the Christians in face of death and torture.[3] And that courage must have been the starting point of many con-

---

[1] Nilsson, *Gesch.*, II, p. 682.

[2] *Anth. Pal.*, 10.82. Neoplatonism continued to be taught by pagans at Athens down to 529, but when Synesius visited that city he could find only the 'husk' of its former intellectual life (*Epist.* 136).

[3] Lucian, *Peregr.*, 13; M. Ant., 11.3; Walzer, *Galen*, p. 15; Origen, *c. Cels.*, 8.65. Cf. also Epictetus, 4.7.6.

versions (Justin's is one example).[1] We know from modern experience of political martyrdoms that the blood of the martyrs really *is* the seed of the Church, always provided that the seed falls on suitable ground and is not sown too thickly. But pagan martyrs under Christian rule were few—not because Christianity was more tolerant, but because paganism was by then too poor a thing to be worth a life.

There were, of course, other reasons for the success of Christianity. I will not discuss the intrinsic merits of the Christian creed; but I will end this chapter by mentioning briefly some of the psychological conditions which favoured its growth and contributed to its victory.

In the first place, its very exclusiveness, its refusal to concede any value to alternative forms of worship, which nowadays is often felt to be a weakness, was in the circumstances of the time a source of strength. The religious tolerance which was the normal Greek and Roman practice had resulted by accumulation in a bewildering mass of alternatives. There were too many cults, too many mysteries, too many philosophies of life to choose from: you could pile one religious insurance on another, yet not feel safe.[2] Christianity made a clean sweep. It lifted the burden of freedom from the shoulders of the individual: one choice, one irrevocable choice, and the road to salvation was clear. Pagan critics might mock at Christian intolerance, but in an age of anxiety any

---

[1] Justin, *Apol. ii*, 12.
[2] Cf. Festugière, *Révélation*, I, pp. 10–14; and for the accumulation of rites the case of Fabia Aconia Paulina, wife of a fourth-century proconsul, who was an initiate of Eleusis, Lerna, Aegina and Isis, had received the taurobolium, and was in addition hierophant of Hecate (*C.I.L.*, VI, 1780=*I.L.S.*, 1260).

'totalist' creed exerts a powerful attraction: one has only to think of the appeal of communism to many bewildered minds in our own day.

Secondly, Christianity was open to all. In principle, it made no social distinctions; it accepted the manual worker, the slave, the outcast, the ex-criminal; and though in the course of our period it developed a strong hierarchic structure, its hierarchy offered an open career to talent.[1] Above all, it did not, like Neoplatonism, demand education. Clement might smile at the quaint beliefs of the *simpliciores*, Origen might declare that true knowledge of God was confined to 'a very few among the few';[2] but the notion of 'Pass and Honours standards in the service of God' (as Arthur Nock once phrased it) was originally foreign to the spirit of Christianity, and on the whole remained so. In the second century and even in the third the Christian Church was still largely (though with many exceptions) an army of the disinherited.[3]

[1] Cf. Momigliano, *Conflict*, pp. 9–11. Origen recognises that in his day the priesthood is beginning to be viewed as a career, and one capable of attracting the ambitious (*c. Cels.*, 3.9). And he claims that in cities like Athens and Alexandria the administration of the Church, though by no means faultless, compares favourably with the civic administration (*ibid.*, 3.30).

[2] Origen, *De oratione*, 24.2. He was not, however, indifferent to the needs of the masses: 'those who pay attention only to people educated in learning and scholarship confine to a very limited and narrow circle what should be of benefit to the community' (*c. Cels.*, 6.1).

[3] Cf. the testimony of Justin, *Apol. ii*, 10.8; Athenagoras, *Leg.*, 11.3; Tatian, *Orat.*, 32.1; Min. Felix, *Oct.*, 8.4; 12.7. Origen admits (*c. Cels.*, 1.27) that the great majority of Christians are 'vulgar and illiterate persons', but implies that the same might be said of pagans. Even at the end of the third century Christianity 'was still largely confined to the middle and lower classes and had made little impression on the aristocracy' (A. H. M. Jones in Momigliano, *Conflict*, p. 37). But there were of course, and had long been, important exceptions (cf. Harnack, *Mission*, II, pp. 36–42): Cyprian, *Epist.* 80.1, refers to special measures taken against Christian senators and *equites*; and Clement's *Paidagogos* was certainly written for the well-to-do.

Thirdly, in a period when earthly life was increasingly devalued and guilt-feelings were widely prevalent, Christianity held out to the disinherited the conditional promise of a better inheritance in another world. So did several of its pagan rivals.[1] But Christianity wielded both a bigger stick and a juicier carrot. It was accused of being a religion of fear, and such it no doubt was in the hands of the rigorists. But it was also a religion of lively hope, whether in the crude terms described for example by Papias,[2] or in the rationalised versions offered by Clement and Origen. Porphyry remarked, as others have done since, that only sick souls stand in need of Christianity.[3] But sick souls were numerous in our period: Peregrinus and Aelius Aristides are not isolated freaks; Porphyry himself had been sufficiently sick to contemplate suicide, and there is evidence for thinking that in these centuries a good many persons were consciously or unconsciously in love with death.[4] For such men the chance of martyrdom,

---

[1] Cf. A. D. Nock, *Harv. Theol. Rev.*, 25 (1932), pp. 344–54.

[2] According to Clement many Christians are actuated (wrongly) by fear of punishment and hope of reward (*Strom.*, 7.69.8). For Papias cf. Iren., *Haer.*, 5.33.3 f., and Eus., *Hist. Eccl.*, 3.39.12; and for the religion of fear, the terrible threats uttered by the *prophetai* known to Celsus (*c. Cels.*, 7.9).

[3] Porph., *Adv. Christ.*, fr. 87. For his own μελαγχολικὴ νόσος see *Vit. Plot.*, 11.11 ff.

[4] The frequency of voluntary martyrdom among Christians is attested by Lucian (*Peregr.*, 13, 'most of them give themselves up voluntarily'), by Celsus (Origen, *c. Cels.*, 8.65), and by Clement, who says (as Julian did later, *Epist.* 89 b Bidez–Cumont) that such people act from a deathwish, θανατῶντες, (*Strom.*, 4.17.1). It is interesting that Epictetus (1.9.11) knows of such a deathwish among young pagans and feels obliged to restrain it, and that Seneca speaks of 'affectus qui multos occupavit, libido moriendi' (*Epist.* 24.25). The pathological nature of the craving for martyrdom seems evident in the wild language of Ignatius, *Ad Rom.*, 4. Healthier motives can be suggested for the mass self-denunciation of Christians described by Tertullian, *Ad Scap.*, 5 which drove the embarrassed magistrate to point out that there were less

carrying with it fame in this world and bliss in the next, could only add to the attractions of Christianity.[1]

But lastly, the benefits of becoming a Christian were not confined to the next world. A Christian congregation was from the first a community in a much fuller sense than any corresponding group of Isiac or Mithraist devotees. Its members were bound together not only by common rites but by a common way of life and, as Celsus shrewdly perceived,[2] by their common danger. Their promptitude in bringing material help to brethren in captivity or other distress is attested not only by Christian writers but by Lucian,[3] a far from sympathetic witness. Love of one's neighbour is not an exclusively Christian virtue,[4] but in our period the Christians appear to have

troublesome ways to die), and for the youthful Origen's desire to suffer along-side his father (Eus., *Hist. Eccl.*, 6.2.3–6). (Was Origen's self-mutilation a surrogate for the martyrdom of which his mother had cheated him, as Cadiou suggests, *Jeunesse d'Origène* (1935), p. 38?) Voluntary martyrdom was, however, in general discouraged by the leaders of the Church (cf. *Mart. Polycarpi*, 4, and Clem., *loc. cit.*). On the whole subject see the perceptive remarks of A. D. Nock, *Conversion*, pp. 197–202, and G. de Ste Croix, *Harv. Theol. Rev.*, 47 (1954), pp. 101–3.

[1] The rewards of martyrdom were considerable. If the 'confessor' withstood the torture and survived, he enjoyed high prestige among his fellow-Christians; if he perished, he could expect to become the object of a cult and to have a privileged position among the dead. According to Tertullian (*De anima*, 55) only martyrs will attain to Paradise before the Second Coming.

[2] *C. Cels.*, 1.1.

[3] *Peregr.*, 12 f.

[4] I do not understand Pohlenz's assertion that love of one's neighbour was something 'hitherto unknown in the ancient world' (*Die Stoa* (1948), p. 407). Cf. e.g. Pliny, *N.H.*, 2.7.18, 'deus est mortali iuvare mortalem'; M. Ant., 7.13, we should love one another 'from the heart'; 7.22, 'it is the proper quality of a man to love even those who err'; Porph., *Ad Marc.*, 35, philanthropy the foundation of piety; and the passages quoted and discussed by A. Dihle, *Die Goldene Regel* (1962), pp. 61–71, 117–27. On pagan philanthropic institutions see H. Bolkestein, *Wohltätigkeit und Armenpflege* (1939). But in the pagan world of the third century philanthropy was preached more often than it was practised. It was a world where, as Rostovtzeff said, 'hatred and envy

practised it much more effectively than any other group.
The Church provided the essentials of social security: it
cared for widows and orphans, the old, the unemployed,
and the disabled; it provided a burial fund for the poor
and a nursing service in time of plague.[1] But even more
important, I suspect, than these material benefits was the
sense of belonging which the Christian community could
give. Modern social studies have brought home to us the
universality of the 'need to belong' and the unexpected
ways in which it can influence human behaviour, particularly among the rootless inhabitants of great cities. I
see no reason to think that it was otherwise in antiquity:
Epictetus has described for us the dreadful loneliness that
can beset a man in the midst of his fellows.[2] Such loneliness must have been felt by millions—the urbanised
tribesman, the peasant come to town in search of work,
the demobilised soldier, the rentier ruined by inflation,
and the manumitted slave. For people in that situation
membership of a Christian community might be the only
way of maintaining their self-respect and giving their
life some semblance of meaning. Within the community
there was human warmth: some one was interested in
them, both here and hereafter. It is therefore not surprising that the earliest and the most striking advances of

reigned everywhere: the peasants hated the landowners and the officials, the
city proletariat hated the city bourgeoisie, the army was hated by everybody'
(*Social and Economic History of the Roman Empire*, p. 453). Christianity was the
one force which could effectively bring the jarring elements together: hence
its attractiveness to Constantine.

[1] See especially Aristides, *Apol.*, 15.7–9 Goodspeed; Justin, *Apol. i*, 67.6;
Dionysius of Corinth (*c.* 160) *apud* Eus., *Hist. Eccl.*, 4.23.10. Harnack, *Mission*,
I, pp. 147–98, gives a full and impressive survey.

[2] Epict., 3.13.1–3.

Christianity were made in the great cities—in Antioch, in Rome, in Alexandria. Christians were in a more than formal sense 'members one of another': I think that was a major cause, perhaps the strongest single cause, of the spread of Christianity.[1]

[1] Cf. A.-J. Festugière, *Rev. de Théol. et de Phil.* (1961), p. 31: 'S'il n'y avait eu cela, le monde serait encore païen. Et le jour où il n'y aura plus cela, le monde redeviendra païen.' Julian seems to have been of a like opinion: he attributes the success of Christianity to 'their philanthropy towards strangers, their care for the burial of the dead, and the pretended strictness of their way of life' (*Epist.* 84 a Bidez–Cumont, 429 d: cf. also above, p. 27).

INDEX

Index

Index

Epicureans, 56
Epiphanius, 64
eros, 89 f.
Essenes, 31
eternity, *see* Aion
ethics, pagan and Christian, 32, 75, 119 f.
Eusebius, 33, 115, 125
Evangelium Veritatis, see Gospel of Truth
exhibitionism, 61
exorcism, 68 n. 1
extra-sensory perception, 55 n. 2

Fabia Aconia Paulina, 133 n. 1
Fate, 13–15
father-image, 20, 45, 63, 78
Fathers, Apostolic, 105; Desert, 30 f., 33, 42 n. 4
Festugière, A.-J., 3, 22, 31, 41 n. 1, 76, 93, 100, 138 n. 1
finger-sacrifice, 43
Firmilian, 66
flagellation, 60, 63
Forrest Reid, 82 f.
Franz, Marie-Louise von, 50 n. 2, 52 n. 3
Freud, Sigmund, 5, 28, 82 n. 2, 88 n. 4, 91 n. 2, 131 n. 3
Fritz, K. von, 60 n. 1
Fromm, Erich, 4 n. 2, 88 n. 4
Fronto, 112

Galen, 32, 45, 105, 121, 132
Galerius, 108
Gellius, Aulus, 61 f.
Gennadius, 46
glossolalia, *see* tongues
Gnosticism, 4, 13–20, 24–6, 58 n. 2, 73, 77, 79, 88, 107 n. 2, 113 n. 2, 130; definition of, 18 n. 2; Gnostic frescoes, 101 n. 1; *see also under individual names*
God, knowledge of, 87, 92; nature of, 118; 'second God', 119; *see also* monotheism, mystical experience

gods, Christian view of, 117; dying, 119 n. 1; mythological, 38; planetary, 13–15; *see also theos*
Golden Verses, 28
Gorer, Geoffrey, 39
Gospel of the Egyptians, 33 n. 1
Gospel of Eve, 73
Gospel of Thomas, 30 n. 1, 51 n. 1, 73 n. 4
Gospel of Truth, 9 n. 4, 16, 96 n. 1
grace, 76 f., 88–90, 98 f.
Grant, Dr and Mrs Michael, ix
Grant, R. M., 16 n. 3, 125 n. 3
Greenslade, S. L., 65
Gregory of Nyssa, 10 f., 46, 72, 74, 88 n. 2, 89 n. 2, 131; mysticism of, 98 f.
guilt-feelings, 20, 35, 42, 43 n. 2, 62 f., 135
Guitton, J., 25 n. 1

Hadot, Pierre, ix, 77 n. 3, 85 n. 2
Harnack, A. von, 118 n. 3, 123 n. 2, 126 n. 4, 137 n. 1
heaven, voyage to, 7
Helen, 19 n. 3
Hell, 129, 131
Heracleon, 16, 130 n. 2
Hermas, 58, 104
Hermetica, 15 f., 24, 30 n. 1, 74, 76 f., 82 f., 92, 93 n. 1, 122 f.
hermits, pagan and Jewish, 31 n. 3
Herodes Atticus, 61, 63
Hierocles, 109, 126 n. 4
Holl, K., 31
Holy Spirit, 49, 59, 65–8; *see also pneuma*
Homer, 100 f., 130 f.
homoiosis, 75 f.
Huxley, Aldous, 87

Iamblichus, 17, 22 f.
identity, crisis of, 29 n. 1, 44 f., 76–8; reciprocal, 72–4
Ignatius, 52, 67, 135 n. 4
incarnation, *see* souls

Index

Ephesians, 15; 1 Timothy, 58 n. 2; 1 John, 16; *see also* Paul, St

Nilsson, M. P., 1 f., 70 n. 2, 132

Nock, A. D., 3, 60 n. 2, 119 n. 2, 134

noesis, 87

Norden, E., 22 n. 1

Numenius, 14, 23 n. 1, 24–6, 93 f., 96, 100, 101 n. 1, 130 n. 2

Old Testament, 35, 71, 126 f.; Genesis, 15, 17, 76; Psalms, 76; Song of Songs, 98; Daniel, 127; Joel, 39

One, the, 84, 88–90

Ophites, 73

oracles, 54–8, 107 f.; *see also* Chaldaean Oracles

Origen, 24, 29 n. 3, 32 f., 46, 67 n. 4, 74, 76 n. 4, 89 n. 2, 93 n. 2, 104, 106 f., 110, 134 f.; on astrology, 15; *contra Celsum*, 112–14, 116–20, 124–6; on creation, 17; on decay of world, 12 n. 1; *ekstasis* in, 71 n. 4; mysticism in, 97 f.; on *pistis*, 122; *De principiis*, 127–32; theology of, 117–19

Orphic, teaching, 23, 122

Otto, Rudolf, 80 n. 1

pacifism, 114

paganism, decline of, 109, 132

Palladas, 11 f., 132

pantheism, 73 f.

Papias, 135

papyri, 57; magical, 72 f.

Paradise, Earthly, 129

Parke, H. W., ix

Paul, St, 17 f., 20, 35, 58, 75, 96 f., 119 n. 2, 121, 123 n. 2, 126, 130

Pepuza, 65 f.

Peregrinus, 59–63

Perpetua, St, 47–53, 116

persecutions, *see* Christians

Persia, 14, 16

Peter, St, 39

Pétrement, S., 18

philanthropy, 27, 136–8

Philo of Byblos, 127

Philo Judaeus, 33 n. 3, 71 f., 76, 94 f.

Philostratus, 34 n. 1

phragmos, 19

pistis, 120–3

Pistis Sophia, 73

planets, *see* gods

Plato, 6, 8 f., 10, 12, 14, 21–3, 25, 37, 75, 80, 84, 87, 89 n. 2, 93, 96

Platonism, 13, 21–3, 91 f.; Christian, 118, 127–30; *see also* Neoplatonism

'Platonopolis', 27 n. 1

Pliny the Younger, 105, 110, 112 f.

Plotinus, 12, 20, 22, 27, 29, 123 n. 2, 125 n. 5, 128, 130 n. 1; on astrology, 15; on divinisation, 74 f.; *ekstasis* in, 72; and Gnosticism, 25 n. 5, 79, 95 f.; and Gregory of Nyssa, 98 f.; on human life, 10; on incarnation of souls, 24–6; and Judaism, 94–6; on Matter, 14; mysticism in, 78, 81, 83–91; and Numenius, 94, 96; on personal identity, 77 n. 3

Plutarch, 4, 16, 35

pneuma, 54 n. 1, 58, 76 n. 5; *see also* Holy Spirit

pneumatikoi, 54

Pohlenz, M., 136 n. 4

Porphyry, 11, 17, 30 n. 1, 56, 74 f., 84, 120 n. 1, 131; on Christianity, 107–9, 112, 115, 118, 125–7, 135; on *pistis*, 122 f.

Poseidonius, 22 n. 1, n. 5

Priscilla, 64

Proclus, 5, 23, 123

Prodicus, the Gnostic, 107 n. 2

progress after death, 129

prophecy, fulfilment of, 49, 126

prophetai, 53–68, 107, 125

prophetesses, 64 f.

Puech, H.-C., 70 n. 2, 85 n. 2

Pythagoras, 14

Index

GREEK HISTORY AND LITERATURE IN
NORTON PAPERBOUND EDITIONS